YOUR HIDDEN SKILLS:

Clues to Careers and Future Pursuits

YOUR HIDDEN SKILLS:

Clues to Careers and Future Pursuits

HENRY G. PEARSON

Mowry Press
Wayland, Massachusetts
1981

Dedicated to

Paul Pigors, Professor Emeritus,
Department of Industrial Relations,
Massachusetts Institute of Technology

and

Roland Darling
Founder of Forty Plus
and
Career Information Center,
Northeastern University

Pioneers in linking the worlds
of education and work

Contents

Preface and Acknowledgements

The basic philosophies of this book derive from two innovators, Bernard Haldane and Edwin H. Land. In the 1940s and '50s Haldane developed his concepts of self-assessment and individual initiative, described them in his writings, and implemented them in the career counseling service that bears his name. Over the same period Dr. Land introduced his doctrines of self-management and individual development which by the mid-50s had resulted in the establishment of an "office of career growth" encompassing education and career counseling for Polaroid employees.

In 1971 — with the encouragement of Walter Jabs — Gladys Bishop and I, both in the Polaroid career office, experimented with a new form of industrial counseling, the Career Direction Workshop. It was modeled on a program designed for Columbia University students by Saul Gruner, of New York City, and Richard M. Gummere Jr., of the university's Career Advising Office, using Haldane's principles of enjoyable achievements and transferable skills.

Following my retirement from Polaroid Corporation in 1973, I began applying the same principles and techniques we had used in industry to schools, colleges, and groups of adults seeking career changes or planning retirement.

I acknowledge the influence of other sources in the field of transferable skills, especially those ideas of Richard N. Bolles, John C. Crystal, Howard E. Figler, Richard Gummere, and the National Center for Research in Vocational Education.

I also appreciate the help of friends and family who read and critiqued all or part of the manuscript. They include Annie W. Allen, Lynwood Bryant, Thomas Dorney, Joel Evett, Stephen Fischer, Shirley Frobes, Richard Gummere, Constance Horwitz,

Edward Kiradjieff, Frank Kirk, Richard Kriebel, Garth Mangum, Cecily Patton, Anne Pearson, Mowry Pearson, Peggy Pearson, Theodore Pearson, William Phillips, John Putnam, Claire Sheff, Laurel and David Smuckler, Kirsten Stromberg, Carl Sykes, Elizabeth Very, and Fritz Walther.

A self-published book is a cooperative effort. Each person makes a special contribution that illuminates the whole. Such contributors are Barbara Gregory, cover design; Carol Kassabian, early typing; Lucinda Parker, art work: and Jane Peppler, design and production. To all go my thanks.

I especially want to thank Dolly Bryant, of South Tamworth, N.H., for her thoughtful and creative editing. And finally I am grateful to my wife, Eleanor, who during the five-year process typed and re-typed while contributing cogent editorial ideas and improvements.

Wayland, Massachusetts
September 1, 1980   H. G. P.

Introduction

All of us have skills hidden away we are not fully aware of. We may have overlooked or not even known about them. Or we may use them so frequently and effortlessly that we take them for granted, and so they go unnoticed. Yet when we uncover these skills we find them to be effective and satisfying guides to our future. And what pleasure in their discovery!

How can it be that you and I do not know these important secrets about ourselves, especially when something good is at stake? Are there any clues for solving this mystery?

Like any detective, you first need to ask yourself the right questions. As simple as that. And the reason you have not done this to date is that your parents, teachers, professors, and bosses have never passed on the questions to you. Alas, these very people who were eager to help you develop may not have known the questions either.

This is too bad. Simply because you lacked some basic tips you are not exploiting those hidden catalysts — the skills that might give you greater satisfaction and enjoyment in the things you do.

That's what this book is for. It tells you the *questions* you should ask yourself to determine what your hidden skills are. It's an odd book that way; most "how to" books tell you all the *answers*. This book does the opposite. It tells you only the questions to ask, and *you* give the answers. Why shouldn't you? You are the world's authority on yourself.

Why all this emphasis on skills? You may have heard that your personality is the most important consideration, or that you really can't decide your future until you establish your values and aims in life. True, these are important, but they must come *after* you assess your skills. Here is why.

All careers, jobs, and other pursuits, paid or unpaid, require skills. You can't do anything without them. In this book I talk about two kinds of skills.

One kind is based on knowledge, know-how, and specialized subject matter. These are the skills associated with fields of knowledge, such as engineering, interior decorating, coal mining, languages, sewing, or, for instance, those which carpentry involves — planing, sawing, and chiseling. The skills used in these disciplines are already well-advertised because our education and work systems are based on them.

The other kind of skills is hidden. Yet you use many of them every day in every form of activity. For the most part they are neither formally taught nor publicized, and that is why they are the subject of this book.

The discovery of these hidden skills and matching them to all kinds of activity, especially work, is the heart of the process which this book describes. The more you learn about this linkage, the easier it will be to find the activity that will give you satisfaction and enjoyment.

This process of discovery and matching I call the *Direction Searchway,* or *Searchway* for short. That means you are going to learn a *way* to *search* for a *direction.* The *Searchway* is a compass to find your direction toward a career, job, or any non-work or unpaid activity. Your age or present level of experience does not matter. This process is described in Part I, Chapters 1 through 7.

Usually you read a book by yourself, and when you've finished, you put it down and are through. But if it's a book like this, it is not much use to you unless you do something further about it. For instance, if you're reading a book on car repair, you also need to practise what you've learned on a car itself. In the same way, the *Searchway* requires you to practise what you've learned on YOU. There are no tools or equipment handy, just yourself.

This is where you're going to have to *ask yourself the questions and answer them yourself.* This is difficult for most people; here's the way to find out if you can or cannot. When you read a textbook, you often find a set of questions at the end of each chapter. Are you the type of person who actually answers these on paper with pencil? Or are you the kind who skims through them ("Oh yes, I know the answer to that"), or ignores those questions you cannot respond to?

If you are a conscientious question-answerer, then maybe you can swing using this book alone. But if you're like most of us, you may rationalize that there's no need to answer the questions right away. However, when someone else joins you in asking the questions, you cannot avoid replying.

That's why I suggest, even though you are the one answering the questions, that you involve some other people, and together follow the steps outlined in the *Searchway*. In the book I simulate a group in which you and I and another person are participating.

Here is the strategy: look over the next seven chapters and familiarize yourself with the general approach. Then invite one or two people (including, perhaps, a counseling type of person) to form a group with you. Then together plunge in and follow the process step by step. I know this is asking a lot to expect you to find someone else to share it with, but I can assure you from experience that you will learn it more effectively.

The group simulated in the *Searchway* includes a character whom you can follow through the entire process. This person happens to be a young adult who is making some career decisions and may seem to you to be somewhat "made up." That is intentional. The character has no sex indicated and is created to illustrate the points being made, not the complicated rational and emotional responses an actual person might give.

If you are older or younger, you may think this case has no bearing on your situation. Or it may focus too heavily on work, whereas you are looking forward to immediate educational or unpaid activities. Don't worry. The principles of searching for hidden skills are so basic that they can be applied to all ages, races, both sexes, and to people at most levels of schooling and experience.

The *Searchway* is like a catalytic compass to point and launch you in a new direction. It does not try to instruct you in details of job hunting. There are already books on this subject — compiling prospect lists, telephoning, writing letters and resumes, and negotiating pay. They are listed at the end of Chapter 7.

If you are not a career seeker or changer at the moment, you may not want to complete all the steps in Chapters 6 and 7 that describe testing out sample jobs. Or if you are a homemaker looking to the very distant future, you may want to stop after Chapter 3. If you chiefly want to expand the use of your skills on your present job, the first two chapters may be enough. In short, you can use the *Searchway* flexibly.

Finally, the *Searchway* is not a "how to" book that ends happily with a cake baked, bookcase built, or garden grown. It is a *how to learn* book. But learning how to learn does not guarantee instant success. Learning to write does not produce an instant Hemingway; nor does learning to fly produce a Lindbergh. I cannot guarantee that if you follow the process you will necessarily discover the perfect solution for you as though a light in a dark room had been switched on. I can promise, though, that you will generate good ideas that you can capitalize on now or later, and that you'll learn a process that you can use for your searches anytime in the future.

Having read thus far you may feel as though you want to see examples of how the *Searchway* has worked for others before you embark on it yourself. If so, turn to one of the chapters in Part II. There, in Chapters 8 to 14, you will find ways that people of various ages have used the process during junior and senior high school, college, adult work life, and pre-retirement years.

So now to Part I and the *Searchway*.

PART I
The Searchway

In this part, Part I, Chapters 1 through 7, you will learn the process for discovering your hidden skills and matching them to jobs, careers, and other forms of activity. This process is called the *Searchway*. You will find yourself immediately in a group that is actually going through the *Searchway's* 12 "STEPS."

1

The Search For Your Experiences

Welcome to our workshop in the *Searchway*. Meet our friend, Terry Hall, another member of the workshop group. Pull up a chair. Get yourself a pad of ruled paper and a pencil. (Please use pencil because you'll be making plenty of erasures!) Prepare yourself for some homework, too.

I can't ask you to relax, because this workshop is hard work, but I know you can have fun at work. So enjoy it as you go along.

The natural place to search for anything is where we expect it to be. The hunter looks in the woods for deer; the miner in the shaft for gold. If we want a new car we visit a showroom. If we want a book we browse in the library. If we are hunting for a job we are likely to start first by hunting where the jobs are to see what's available. We figure the search for a career is done the same way. We start by looking around to see what careers there are.

This method works reasonably well for most things. As you scan the shelves, showrooms, or shop windows you begin to generate ideas about what it is you really want. Looking at a lot of houses for sale helps you decide what you want and don't want. Reading a movie guide helps you boil down your choices for the evening.

But this method does *not* work as a first step in choosing a career direction. You cannot see a career or price it. Why? Because a career is not made up just of employers, offices, things to learn, money to earn, tasks to perform, that is, things outside of you. A career is made up with *you* as its centerpiece. All these other elements will impinge on you. But you as a person remain the protagonist.

Who you are, therefore, is the most important thing to find out about first. As there is no description of you anywhere, you're going to have to develop one yourself. That's why this process starts out by asking you to describe yourself in terms of your skills and attributes. These are the talents that you carry with you for life (Chapters 1 and 2).

But finding a direction consists of more than discovering your skills. You need also to take into account a wide range of other information about yourself. This includes such things as your priorities in terms of your preferences, goals, wishes, and absolute musts (Chapter 3).

By this time you'll have become knowledgeable enough to look at jobs, careers and other activities in an entirely new way. You'll begin to see how skills are the essentials to look for first when considering a job, and you'll get some practice doing this (Chapter 4).

At this point you can start developing a list of all the things you could do with these skills. The bigger the list the better (Chapter 5). And from it you select one or two that interest you enough to sample and to weigh their pros and cons (Chapter 6).

There are five homework assignments for the career seeker or changer. Allow yourself enough time between sessions to complete the work. Don't rush through in a few days. Try to meet weekly. If you have to stretch, don't let more than two weeks go by. Some people combine some sessions, others take more than five. You are the best judge of that.

There are 12 "STEPS" to the *Searchway*. The first two are:

STEP 1: Listing Your Experiences
STEP 2: Describing Your Experiences

Now we are all set to start.

STEP 1: Listing Your Experiences

Every once in a while we find we've done something that we got a kick out of and thoroughly enjoyed. We look back and can say to ourselves, "Hey, I feel pretty good about that." We all have more of these experiences than we realize, because we usually don't bother to stop and think about how successful we were and that we actually did something well.

These things, or events, or experiences should be —

— something you really enjoyed doing;
— something you feel good about and feel you did pretty well;
— something you're proud of.[1]

They should always include all three criteria. Throughout the *Searchway* I usually refer to these events simply as "experiences."

These experiences can be found in any period or facet of your life. That's why they are often called "life experiences." They may concern family, friends, schoolmates, or colleagues. They may involve sports, hobbies, intellectual and cultural activities. They may be things you did well and enjoyed at home, school, work, or in your community. They may be for pay or for love. You don't have to be an expert. Here are some examples others have volunteered:

Helping a friend	Completing an experiment
Babysitting	Building a garden
Running a meeting	Persuading the boss
Getting a job	Giving a talk
Playing basketball	Fixing up a room
Raising a family	Repairing a car to run
Presenting a report	Handling a complaint
Knitting a sweater	Getting promoted

In every case these were things that people had —

— enjoyed,
— felt good about and did pretty well,
— were proud of.

Can anyone give an example of some experience of their own like this? Terry? (Terry's remarks are always in *italics*.)

Terry: Yes. When I learned to drive and got my license. I like bicycling, too.

Those are good examples. Don't worry if they don't seem important to you now. If they were important at the time and seemed significant to *you*, that's what counts. All our lives parents, teachers, counselors, and bosses tell us what *they* think of our abilities. Parents comment, teachers mark, counselors test, employers appraise. Someone else is always doing the evaluating. Someone is always comparing you to someone else. All very interesting. But when is someone going to ask you what *you* think is important? That's what this STEP 1 is all about.

Are you having trouble thinking up these accomplishments? Yes? Here are some tips. Did you ever take a course that you thoroughly enjoyed and got good marks in? If so, list it. Has there been any part of a job, no matter how slight (say 10 minutes a day only), that you liked and worked well at? What do you do in your free time? When the time seems to be going fast, what are you doing?

GROUP EXERCISE

Now each person start making a list of his or her own. You are going to need at least 10 experiences eventually. Use the STEP 1 form (following) headed, "Listing Your Experiences." Make a photocopy of it if you do not want to mark up the book.

The asterisks below will always indicate a break in which you start doing the exercise. (However, you will probably not be completing it in the group, but at home later on.)

*   *   *   *   *

What about not enjoying some part of the experience? On a bike trip I had a tire blow out. I can't say I liked patching it in the broiling sun.

Right. Sometimes there'll be a part that's not much fun. Getting lost on a walking trip; dealing with a cranky person. But overcoming these obstacles and solving these problems may give you pleasure, too. Terry, will you show us the way your list is shaping up?

STEP 1: Listing Your Experiences

1. Learning to drive

2. Tutoring a friend

3. Bicycle trip

4. Giving a talk

5. Gardening

6. Cafeteria checkout

STEP 1: Listing Your Experiences

1.

2.

3.

4.

5.

6.

7.

8.

9.

10.

STEP 2: Describing Your Experiences

I am going to ask you to describe one of these experiences in detail.[2] It's important that you mention every action you took. Just tell it as though you were telling a story to a child; begin at the beginning and go through to the end. The STEP 2 form, "Describing Your Experiences," you will be using follows. (You'll be using the same form for STEP 3, to be discussed later.)

It will help if Terry describes one first. As Terry talks I will illustrate how to jot down some notes on Terry's STEP 2 form.

STEP 2: Describing Your Experiences	STEP 3: Identifying Your Transkills
LEARNING TO DRIVE	
I WANTED TO LEARN TO DRIVE. EVERYONE DOES. I APPLIED AT A SCHOOL AND TOOK LESSONS FROM AN INSTRUCTOR. TOOK TURNS DRIVING — READ REGULATION BOOK.	
ASKED FRIEND TO TAKE ME OUT DRIVING THO' HE DIDN'T WANT TO. NERVOUS, BUT I GOT OVER IT.	
PASSED — GOT LICENSE	

Good. Now I'm going to call your attention to five questions you must always ask yourself:

Question #1: Did I describe how this event started and who started it? For instance: "My parents asked..."; "I decided..."; "I had been watching..."

Well, I guess I decided myself.

Question #2: Did I do anything to plan or prepare for this event? Yes. In this case Terry studied the manual.

STEP 2: Describing Your
        Experiences

STEP 3: Identifying
        Your Transkills

Question #3: Have I included every detail of the activity itself? Like, "I measured each board..."; "I hit the ball with the bat..."; "I talked with my associates..."

Terry, tell me what you actually do when you drive a car? *I push on the brakes for one thing; also the accelerator. I give hand signals and steer the wheel. Oh, yes. I keep looking around.*

Question #4: How did I interact with other people? Examples: "I showed her how to tend the bees..."; "I got them to agree..."; "I took care of her kids..."

In your case, Terry, you've already mentioned the other people involved, your friend and the inspector.

Question #5: Have I stated any evidence of my success? "My friends said they liked the dress I made..."; "We all got back safely..."

Evidence? I got my license.

It's not always necessary, though, to produce evidence of success. Perhaps you remember enjoying tremendously a walk you took with some friends. No need to prove it was successful. Your own judgment is sufficient.

TIP: If you get bogged down writing a description, keep asking yourself what you actually did to make it happen.[3]

You may wonder why I'm asking you only about things you like and do well. Isn't it important to think about things you dislike and don't do well?

My answer is "No," not at this stage. Too much of our planning focuses on what we cannot do: "I'm no good at math;" "I didn't go to college;" "I don't have any hobbies;" "I haven't had the experience;" "I lack qualifications."

We spend more time analyzing our weaknesses than our strengths. We seldom say to ourselves (let alone to others), "Hey, I'm pretty good at meeting people;" "I really got that car going and I enjoyed doing it;" "I got a kick out of licking that problem." Yet these are just the kinds of successes we should pinpoint in order to find out what talents we use.

GROUP EXERCISE

Now you should each have a chance to tell a similar story to someone else. (If there are more than three or four of you, make up two sub-groups.)

Each of you has 5 minutes in which to tell the others about

some experience you really enjoyed. If you are A, allow enough time for B and C to question you about the story. Make sure the five key questions are asked.

After 5 minutes, B takes over and A and C listen and ask questions; and so on through C's turn.

*   *·   *   *   *

YOUR HOMEWORK

Complete your list of experiences on your STEP 1 form (page 5). Then write descriptions of at least three of them on the left side of your STEP 2 form (page 7). Don't worry about the order or spelling. Just get the ideas down. Outline if you want.

Question. What's the purpose of writing out all these stories, anyway?

These stories are the basic information you need in order to identify what your skills are. You cannot guess at your skills. You need first-hand reports on what you actually do when you are enjoying yourself.

If you like, take a look at the next chapter and see how you will be identifying skills. By the way, if your group is moving fast on STEPS 1 and 2, and you have more time at this session, you may want to proceed to STEP 3. There is no rule that you must follow the homework breaks rigidly.

FOOTNOTES

1. Bernard Haldane, *How to Make a Habit of Success* (New York: Acropolis, 1975), p. 5
2. Bernard Haldane, *How to Make a Habit of Success*, p. 50.
3. Richard N. Bolles, *What Color is Your Parachute?* (Berkeley: Ten Speed Press, 1973), p. 184.

2

The Search For Your Transkills

Each of you has now completed two or three written accounts of some experiences that you've enjoyed, done well, and are proud of (your copies of STEP 2, page 7). You are going to use one of these in the next STEP, STEP 3.

This STEP involves finding the skills you used when you had each of these experiences. As I mentioned in the Introduction, there are two kinds of skills. The first kind is based on knowledge, know-how, or subject-matter. Some examples: computer programming, navigating, playing soccer, translating French. These skills are already well-known to most people, and you already know which are yours.

The second kind, the skills that you are not so aware of, are your aptitudes (like *mechanical* or *reasoning*); your abilities (like *being artistic*); your attributes or characteristics or traits (like *being persuasive, assertive, helpful*). I have found no single satisfactory word to describe all these factors that make up a personal experience. So I have coined the word "transkills" to cover them all. Transkills are not confined to a special field of knowledge, but can be transferred from one form of activity to the next.

STEP 3: Identifying Your Transkills

Your task now is to analyze the description of your experience for the transkills you used. Look for some action words in your description. For instance, if your experience was playing basketball and you described shooting baskets, then one of the transkills you use shooting baskets is *coordinating eyes and body*.

It's not easy, though, to spot all the transkills yourself. You need other people's ideas and some aids. On the page that follows is a list of commonly-used transkills. I call it the "Transkills Finder."

There are 168 words representing transkills in 22 groups. These groups are mainly for convenience in presenting the words all together on one page. Some words fit just as well into other groups. For instance, *touching* under the heading THE SENSES could also be classified under THE BODY; *performing* could come under ARTISTIC ABILITIES.

Because you have your own special associations with these words, you should respect your groupings, not mine. Also, don't feel you have to stick to these exact words. If you have a better one, use it. Note that the headings themselves can be used as transkills, too.

Let me explain the use of the Transkills Finder by taking Terry's Experience #1, "Learning to Drive," as an example. Terry, turn back to your STEP 2 and STEP 3 form (page 6).

Now go through the Transkills Finder and look for words that apply to "Learning to Drive." As you find them, enter them in the STEP 3 column approximately opposite the action to which they apply.

STEP 2: Describing Your Experiences	STEP 3: Identifying Your Transkills
LEARNING TO DRIVE	
I WANTED TO LEARN TO DRIVE. EVERYONE DOES.	Setting goals
I APPLIED AT A SCHOOL AND TOOK LESSONS FROM AN INSTRUCTOR - TOOK TURNS DRIVING	Initiating Listening, following instructions Learning
READ REGULATION BOOK	Studying/reading memorizing
ASKED FRIEND TO TAKE ME OUT DRIVING THO' HE DIDN'T WANT TO.	Persuading
NERVOUS, BUT I GOT OVER IT.	
PASSED - GOT LICENSE	Getting results

The Transkills Finder

WORDS
Reading
Writing
Conversing
Interviewing
Reporting information

NUMBERS
Calculating
Working with figures
Estimating
Handling money
Buying/shopping
Economizing

ARTISTIC ABILITIES
Using artistic talents
Being creative
Sensing beauty through
  eyes/ears
Interpreting feelings,
  ideas, sights, sounds

**MECHANICAL/TECHNI-
CAL ABILITIES**
Making machines &
  mechanical things work
Applying knowledge to
  technical things

THE BODY
Coordinating eyes/body
Being physically active
Applying strength
Moving around
Coordinating eyes/
  hands
Using hands
Operating things/tools
Using fingers
Building/making
Repairing/fixing

THE SENSES
Observing
Examining
Inspecting
Visualizing
Listening/hearing
Touching/feeling

THE MIND
Original Thinking
Coming up with ideas
Using imagination
Improvising/inventing
Conceptualizing
Intuitive Thinking
Sizing up
Having insight

Gaining Knowledge
Learning
Investigating/
  researching
Memorizing
Recalling
Analyzing
Evaluating

Thinking Ahead
Planning/goal setting
Using foresight
Being logical/reasoning
Problem solving/deci-
  sion making involving:
  people
  information
  things
  ideas

BEING ORGANIZED
Organizing
Starting things up
Scheduling
Following up
Persisting
Getting result(s)
Meeting demands:
  quantity
  quality
  deadlines
Attending to detail
Being thorough/careful
Being accurate/exact
Using system
Being neat/orderly
Using clerical skills
Keeping records
Maintaining routines

SELF-DIRECTING
Asserting self
Taking risks
Taking on responsibility
Being independent
Being self-disciplined
Keeping cool
Developing self

**RELATIONS w/OUTDOOR
& NATURAL WORLD**
Taking care of living
  things
Raising/training living
  things
Dealing with elements/
  nature

**RELATIONS WITH
OTHERS**
Persuading
Influencing
Selling
Promoting
Negotiating
Bargaining

Performing for Others
Entertaining
Speaking
Using showmanship
Demonstrating
Helping Others
Being of service
Serving
Volunteering
Doing favors
Meeting others' physical
  needs
Being sensitive
Guiding/advising
Encouraging
Being patient

Taking Direction
Getting & delivering
  things
Adapting to others
Following directions
Instructing
Training/coaching
Teaching
Explaining
Informing
Leading
Directing others
Managing
Motivating
Being reponsible for
  others' actions
Associating
Cooperating
Sharing
Contacting
Consulting with
Being tactful
Socializing
Being friendly
Making joint effort (2)
Making team effort
Being Competitive
Winning
Contending

I had no idea there could be so many in a thing like learning to drive a car.

That's because you take it for granted. Most everyone learns to drive. But not everyone enjoyed it that much. You did. There's the difference. And because you did, you enjoyed the transkills you used.

The importance of these transkills to you right now is that you are acquiring a new vocabulary for all your activities. A specific action, "steering the wheel," converts into a much broader term, *operating things with hands.* A narrow term, like "pushing on the brakes," associated only with driving a car, escalates into a generic term, *coordinating eyes/body,* that has universal use.

Be sure to read over and get acquainted with each of the 168 words in the Transkills Finder. These are the terms we shall constantly be utilizing in the two aspects of your search: first, in recognizing the transkills you already possess, and later in spotting transkills needed in the new careers you are considering. Once you identify your own transkills they become your set of tags that enable you to match up those which your known past may have in common with your possible future.

GROUP EXERCISE

In your sub-groups, now, let A tell about an experience he or she wrote up on the STEP 2 form (page 7). Then, using the Transkills Finder, have B and C help A to identify the transkills and jot them down in the STEP 3 column. This should take about 10 minutes. Next B describes an experience and A and C help with the transkills. Finally C has a turn.

*   *   *   *   *

Let's go on to Terry's description of Experience #2, which is "Tutoring a friend," and identify the transkills.

STEP 2: Describing Your Experiences	STEP 3: Identifying Your Transkills
Tutoring a friend	
My classmate was failing in English. I offered to coach him.	Goal setting, Being sensitive, Volunteering, Helping others, Coaching, Initiating.
We worked out what help he needed and how much.	Making a joint effort, Analysing, Evaluating, Planning, Scheduling
I made up assignments. I corrected his grammar + spelling.	Observing, Examining, Writing, Conversing, Attention to detail, Reading
We met 2 hours 2 nights a week.	Being systematic
He got interested, – did homework – passed exam.	Listening, Motivating others, Getting results.

Note that sometimes you have to read between the lines. For instance, a great many things we do require *planning*. And if you plan, you usually are *analyzing* and *evaluating* the situation first. Yet we tend not to give ourselves credit for these skills because, again, we take them for granted.

REMINDER: You may have your own words that you want to use instead of those in the Transkills Finder. Go right ahead. It's important that they be words that sound right to you and that you can own.

STEP 4: Organizing Your Transkills

As you add more and more experiences — try for 10 — you find that some transkills are repeating themselves in your different experiences; others are appearing for the first time. You need a way to organize this information. The STEP 4 form, "Organizing Your Transkills," (see following pages) will do just that. I will explain it by helping Terry fill it in. (See Terry's STEP 4 form opposite.)

Under the heading, "EXPERIENCES," in the slanting space above #1, write in the title of your #1 experience, "Learning to Drive." Then under "TRANSKILLS" in the left column enter the transkills you used.

Notice that the lines in this column are grouped. As you enter each transkill try to put it in a grouping with other transkills that seem to you to be related. Don't feel that your groupings need to be just like those on the Transkills Finder. Make up your own!

To illustrate: Terry, will you tell us how you are going about entering the transkills for Experience #1?

> *In the first grouping I put coordinating eyes/body and operating things with your hands. Some of the other skills were scattered through the Transkills Finder, but to me they seemed to belong together:*
> *Observing*
> *Reading*
> *Studying*
> *Later I added to this grouping:*
> *Learning*
> *Following instructions*
> *Memorizing*
> *Another pair, initiating and setting a goal, made sense. Then there were two involving other people:*
> *Persuading (my friend to coach me)*
> *Cooperating (with him and also the instructor)*

GROUP EXERCISE

Each person enter the title to his or her Experience #1 in the slanting box on the STEP 4 form, and follow the same procedure Terry did. Be sure to leave plenty of space between groupings.

STEP 4: Organizing Your
         Transkills

EXPERIENCES

LEARNING TO DRIVE

TRANSKILLS	#1	#2	#3	#4	#5	#6	#7	#8
Coordinating eyes/hands	✓							
Operating with hands	✓							

Grouping

TRANSKILLS	#1	#2	#3	#4	#5	#6	#7	#8
Observing carefully	✓							
Studying/Reading	✓							
Learning new	✓							
Following instructions	✓							
Memorizing	✓							

Grouping

TRANSKILLS	#1	#2	#3	#4	#5	#6	#7	#8
Initiating things	✓							
Setting goals	✓							

Grouping

TRANSKILLS	#1	#2	#3	#4	#5	#6	#7	#8
Persuading	✓							
Cooperating	✓							

Grouping

TRANSKILLS	#1	#2	#3	#4	#5	#6	#7	#8

Grouping

STEP 4: Organizing Your Transkills

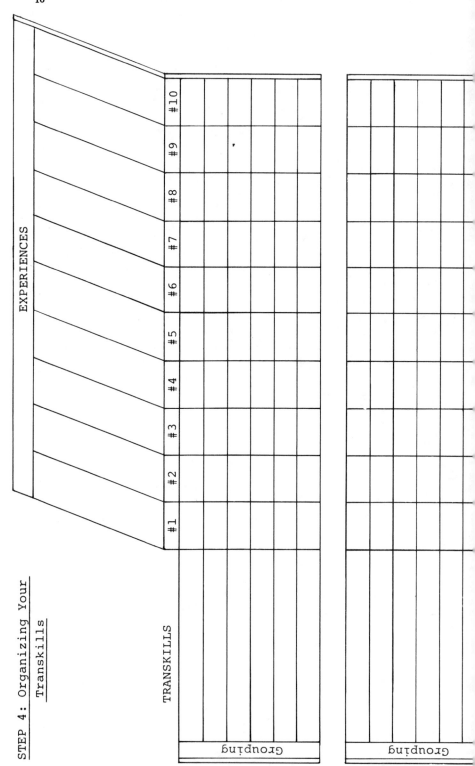

Grouping

Grouping

Grouping

You may eventually need three or more copies of the chart, so make photocopies of it first. Use pencil. You may want to erase.

* * * * *

Terry, will you show us how you entered the transkills for Experience #2, "Tutoring a friend"? (See additions to Terry's STEP 4 form that follows.) I notice you checked quite a few of the same skills as in #1, but you added some new ones.

> Yes, I did a lot of correcting his work. So I called it examining or inspecting. Then I realized these apply to "Learning to drive," (like inspecting the emergency brake). So I checked them off in column #1 also.
>
> In my next grouping I figured I had to use my own ideas; that seemed to go with initiating. Volunteering could have gone with that grouping, but I wanted to put it with transkills I used with people, like cooperating, helping, explaining, teaching.

GROUP EXERCISE

Everyone can go ahead and enter the transkills for his or her experience #2.

* * * * *

YOUR HOMEWORK

Transfer the transkills from your experience #3 on to the STEP 4 chart. After that you won't need to write out experiences #4, 5, 6, etc. You can go directly to the chart and check off the transkills that apply to experiences #4, 5, 6, etc. and add any new skills. Whenever you add a new one to the list, go back to your previous experiences and see if it would apply to them, also.

TIP: Don't worry if the words don't seem to group perfectly; this is a first try. If two words seem pretty much alike, put them both on the same line with a slash (/) between them; or throw one out. . . Use another chart if need be; Terry used two.

* * * * *

STEP 4: Organizing Your
Transkills

EXPERIENCES

TRANSKILLS	#1 LEARNING TO DRIVE	#2 TUTORING A FRIEND	#3	#4	#5	#6	#7	#8
Grouping								
Coordinating eyes/hands	✓							
Operating with hands	✓							
Grouping								
Observing carefully	✓	✓						
Studying/Reading	✓	✓						
Learning new	✓	✓						
Following instructions	✓	✓						
Memorizing	✓	✓						
Examining/Inspecting	✓	✓						
Grouping								
Initiating Things	✓	✓						
Setting goals/Planning	✓	✓						
Coming up with ideas		✓						
Grouping								
Persuading	✓	✓						
Cooperating	✓	✓						
Volunteering		✓						
Helping		✓						
Coaching/Explaining		✓						
Grouping								

STEP 4: Organizing Your Transkills (continued)

The STEP 4 forms you have just completed at home give you a bird's eye view of all the transkills you use when you are doing things you enjoy. You can quickly spot those that you use most frequently. It can be startling to see how often you use a skill that you had not been much aware of.

But frequency is not the whole story. Let's check this out. Terry, when you were learning to drive and coaching your friend, were there any transkills you used but did not particularly enjoy using?

> *Yes. I didn't especially like memorizing the driving regulations or some rules of grammar that I felt I ought to know by heart if I was teaching them.*

So you need to distinguish on the chart the transkills you enjoy using from those you use but do not enjoy. Here's how. Review each transkill and its checkmarks horizontally. Leave those you do not enjoy as they are. Shade in the boxes that have checks representing transkills you enjoy.

On the page that follows take a look at Terry's final STEP 4 form after the shading is completed. The shaded boxes now give a vivid picture of the transkills Terry enjoys and uses most often.

GROUP EXERCISE

Each of you should now proceed to shade the boxes for transkills enjoyed.

*   *   *   *   *

Your chart gives you some idea of the groupings of your transkills. But you probably want a better arrangement that emphasizes the most significant transkills. You certainly want to cut back on the number of words. Here is the process to follow:

1) Find a grouping that has great significance to you, or that is important, or that you enjoy tremendously.

2) From that grouping select a word or two that best represents the grouping. (Terry might pick *studying up* and *learning.*) Write them on a card or slip of paper.

3) Now go to another grouping that is also significant, but is quite different. (Terry might choose *persuading* and *explaining.*) Write them on another card.

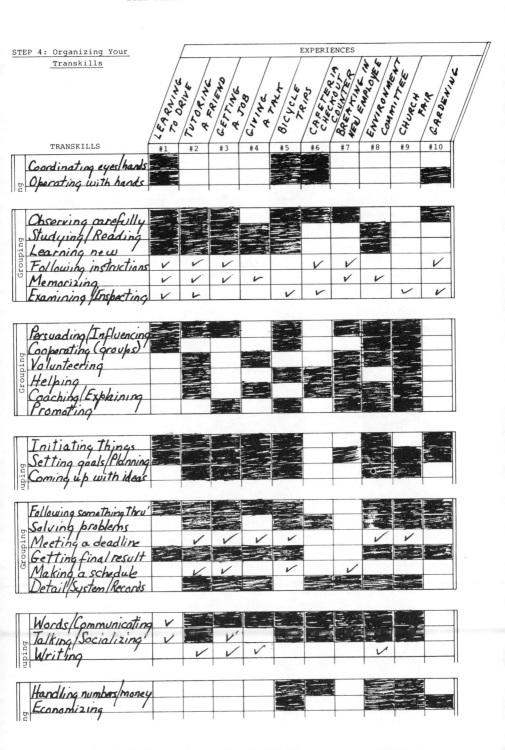

4) Continue to another quite different set of transkills. (Another of Terry's could be *attention to detail* and *systematizing.*) Enter on card.

5) Go on this way until you feel you have covered your significant groupings of transkills, each with a word or two on a card.

6) Now go back and add to each card any other words that you think belong on it. Just don't get too many. The aim is to make you think which of these transkills are top priority.

7) Spread the cards out; move them around. You may see some you want to combine. Or there may be a transkill that deserves a card of its own. Keep combining or eliminating until you have not more than six or eight cards of groupings that represent you and that you feel comfortable with. (Terry's original and revised arrangements of transkill groupings follow.)

Terry's Arrangements of Transkills Groupings

Original Version   Revised Version

Learning new
Studying up → Learning new
Studying up

Getting Things
started - planning
Having ideas → Having ideas - Planning
Starting Things
Follow through w. details
Solving problems

Following Through
with details
Solving problems

Handling money
Economizing → Handling money
Economizing
Keeping records
Numbers

Using words
Talking / Socializing → Communicating
Socializing
Contacting

Volunteering
Helping
Cooperating → Helping others
Cooperating (groups)

Persuading
Promoting → Persuading
Promoting
Explaining

Coaching
Explaining

GROUP EXERCISE

Each of you can now follow the instructions on page 22 and arrange your own transkill grouping cards. Remember, this is only a first try; you will have second thoughts and want to add, subtract, or rearrange the cards later. Compare notes with the others and see if you can explain your groupings to them.

TIP: If you have trouble deciding what words to choose, ask yourself whether or not you would like to use that transkill in the future.

*   *   *   *   *

Once you have these groupings well in mind you have solved the mystery about yourself. The clues are these transferable talent areas. They form the backbone of your own person-description. Now you are ready to move on to gathering information about a different aspect of yourself — that is, what is it you want for yourself and what are your priorities?

RESOURCES

Transferable Skills

Bolles, Richard N. *The Quick Job Hunting Map*, Beginning version. Berkeley: Ten Speed Press, 1977.

Bolles, Richard N. *What Color is Your Parachute*, Berkeley, Ten Speed Press, 1980 edition. Pp. 186-204.

Bolles, Richard N. *The Three Boxes of Life*, Ten Speed Press, 1978. Pp. 132-183 and 204-211.

Crystal, John C. and Richard N. Bolles. *Where Do I Go from Here with my Life?* New York: Seabury, 1974. Pp. 67-70 and 204-209.

Fine, Sidney A. "A Re-examination of 'Transferability of Skills,' Part II," *Monthly Labor Review*, August 1957. Pp. 938-948.

Fine, Sidney A. and Wretha W. Wiley. *An Introduction to Functional Job Analysis*. Kalamazoo, Mich.: W. E. Upjohn Institute, 1971.

Haldane, Bernard. *How to Make a Habit of Success*, Washington, D.C.: Acropolis, 1975 (Original edition 1960). Pp. 51-56.

Pearson, Henry G. "Self-Identification of Talents: First Step to Finding Career Directions," *Vocational Guidance Quarterly*, September 1975. Pp. 20-26.

Pratzner, Frank C. *Occupational Adaptability and Transferable Skills*, Columbus, Ohio: National Center for Research in Vocational Education, Ohio State University, 1978.

3

The Search For Your Priorities

This phase of the *Searchway* helps you identify your personal preferences, wishes, and "musts." From these you determine what your priorities are. Here are the STEPS:

STEP 5: Listing your likes.
STEP 6: Recording your wishes.
STEP 7: Identifying your musts.
STEP 8: Selecting your special knowledge skills.
STEP 9: Summarizing your priorities.

These STEPS help pull together a lot of things you have probably been thinking about and some you have not. *You* are the only person who can determine what your preferences are; what you hope and wish for; and what things you know you must have. Also, for the first time, you are asked about some other kinds of skill — your knowledge-based skills and which ones you want to use in the future.

Finally, you are asked which of all these things are the most important to you, that is, what your priorities are.

You will be working on these STEPS at home. The forms you need for STEPS 5,6,7,8 and 9 are all together at the end of this chapter.

STEP 5: Listing Your Likes

It may help to see how one person went about this task. That's Terry, of course. Jumping ahead, let's pretend Terry has completed all of these steps. Start with Terry's STEP 5.

STEP 5: Listing Your Likes

List about a dozen things you like or like to do, watch, or listen to. They may include things you have liked in the past. (Forget about whether or not you have any skill involved.) In the right column try to state WHY you like them. Then list some places you like and why.

Things I like	Why I like them
Travel	See new Things
Walk in mountains	outdoors + exercise
Reading	relaxing
Meeting people	sociability
Listening to records	music, relaxation
Reading about	action, contests
sports events	

Places and Surroundings I like	Why I like them
Upper Peninsula, Mich.	out of The way
San Francisco	cosmopolitan, variety
Rocky Mountains	outdoors, nature
Restaurants	good food, people

STEP 6: Recording Your Wishes

And here, again, is the way Terry filled in STEP 6.

STEP 6: Recording Your Wishes

* If you did not have any responsibilities or have
  to earn a living, how would you use your time?
  (Exclude complete idleness.)

  Studying people and their customs.

  What appeals to you most about it?

  Meeting and talking with new people.

* What courses would you like to take for fun?

  Gardening.

* If you had $50,000 given you to use on something
  other than yourself or family, how would you spend
  it?

  Probably some environmental organization.

* If you were interviewed by your local newspaper 10
  years from now, what would you like them to report
  about you?

  Important figure in world problems.

* What do you think needs doing in the world?

  Cleaning up man's messes.

  What would YOU actually want to do about it?

  Investigate some phase of it.

* Assuming there were no limitations on you, what
  would be your absolutely ideal, dream occupation?

  Politics.

  What especially appeals to you about it?

  Being of service - being known.

  The space provided is limited. You may want to use
  additional sheets.

STEP 7: Identifying Your Musts

Let me amplify the instructions on the STEP 7 form at the end of this chapter. There are probably some things you want very much in connection with your future job or career — things that you value highly. These vary for different people. Nobody except *you* can say what they are.

Section A of the form asks you to go back to your 10 experiences in STEP 1, page 5. Of each experience ask yourself:

"What was the biggest satisfaction I got out of this experience," OR,

"What was the payoff for me?" OR,

"Why did I do it?"

Here are some examples of satisfactions other people have reported. But don't use them unless they apply to you:

✓   "I got satisfaction from this experience because of —

    — getting recognized,
    — the fun I had,
    — getting something accomplished,
    — doing my duty,
    — winning, or being best,
    — being accepted by others,
    — being of help to someone else."

These satisfactions are also called "values."

Section B asks for any other things you value greatly. For instance, ask yourself whether or not you want to —

    — make a lot of money or enough,
    — be secure or take risks,
    — be out in front or behind the scenes,
    — be your own boss or work in an establishment,
    — live where you are now or elsewhere, etc.

There may be others. But just name those that are *your* values, not other people's; not those that you think you *should* have.

Section C asks you to circle any satisfactions in Sections A and B that you feel are absolutely essential to you in the future. These are your "musts." One way to test for a must is to see if it has been a consistent part of your behavior in the past. In order to claim it as a must, you really ought to have some proof that you act on this value. If you said in Section B that you get satisfaction and value from "service to others," then to claim it as a must, there should be evidence of it among your 10 experiences. If you claim "being your own boss" as a must, check whether you actually have done some things on your own, or whether it is only a wish (perhaps an item for STEP 6). In short, these musts, based on satisfaction and values, should be operational. Here is Terry's semi-completed STEP 7 form.

STEP 7: Identifying Your Musts

A. Review Experience #1 on your Transkills Chart and enter in the left column on the chart below the answer to this question:

"WHAT GAVE ME SATISFACTION IN THIS EXPERIENCE?"

SATISFACTIONS	#1 Learning to drive	#2 Tutoring a friend	#3	#4	#5	#6	#7	#8
Being on my own	✓							
Having status	✓							
Being of service		✓						
Getting recognition	✓	✓						
Accomplish something	✓	✓						
Gaining confidence	✓	✓						
Moving around	✓							

(EXPERIENCES)

Answer the same question for each of the other experiences and check off any words that repeat; add new ones.

B. List any other things that you value greatly or that are important to you (see instructions, page 30). If you have trouble with this, go through your answers to all the WHY questions in STEPS 5 and 6.

Being successful
Getting known
Good pay

C. Circle any of the satisfactions or values in A and B that are absolutely essential to you in the future. These are your MUSTS.

STEP 8: Selecting Your Special Knowledge Skills

The skills we've been talking about up to this point are based on all kinds of life experiences and are transferable. We called them "transkills." Now we are going to investigate the other kind of skill which is based on a particular field of knowledge or which represents some special know-how. These are the skills you often learn in a more formal way as in school or at work. Or the skill may come from some know-how you picked up in a specialized activity. *Knowledge-based skills are not transferable the way transkills are.* Examples would be speaking French, kyacking, astronomy, typing, using a library catalogue, trying a case in court. They require you to learn a body of knowledge that applies to that particular activity. For instance, knowing how to kyack does not help you to know how to type.

Like all rules, there are exceptions. Two kinds of skills that are both knowledge-based and transferable are those dealing with *words* and *numbers.*

Note Terry's special knowledge skills on the STEP 8 form.

STEP 8: Selecting Your Special Knowledge Skills

Jot down any special knowledge, subject matter, or know-how that you have and that you would like to make use of in your future.

Below are listed some areas that might remind you of such knowledge or know-how:

From school: *Course in international relations*

From other courses, seminars, or training:

From paid work:

From non-paid activities or service: *Environmental concerns*

From recreational activities:

From your "experiences" (STEP 1): *Working on environmental problems (Experience # 8)*

STEP 9: Summarizing Your Priorities

One of the aims of the *Searchway* is to try to get you to make some decisions about what is important to you. This is hard, because we often like to hold on to everything. We do not want to make a commitment to priorities. If you feel that way, regard this as an exercise that you can revise at any time.

To get ready to choose your priorities, go back to STEPS 5, 6, 7 and 8 and mark a big [F] opposite any items you would like to see in your future. Then move on to filling out the form.

STEP 9: Summarizing Your Priorities

From each of the previous steps, list the three items most important to you:

From   Most Important Items

STEP 5:   *Outdoor and nature*
(Likes)   *Social activities*
          Seeing new Things
          Cosmopolitan places

STEP 6:   *Environment concerns*
(Wishes) *Politics - service to people*

STEP 7:   *Moving around / travel*
(Musts)   *Good pay*
          Being successful + known

STEP 8:   *Environmental matters*
(Special *International affairs*
Knowledge) *Politics*

These "Most Important Items" are your Priorities.

I seem to be going around and around. The same things keep coming up in this summary.

That's exactly the point. When you report what you really enjoy and want, you keep coming back to a pattern; that's what you're looking for.

GROUP EXERCISE

Members of the group should share a few of the items they have already thought about in connection with STEPS 5 to 9.

YOUR HOMEWORK

Complete the STEP 5 to 9 forms on the next five pages. As you can see, a lot of the thinking about yourself and your future does take place in between these sessions rather than at them! And, of course, complete the arrangement of your transkills groupings (pp. 22 and 24).

This will bring you to a point where you can begin to see what you have accomplished so far in the *Searchway* —

The information you put together on your transkill areas
(STEP 4)

+   The information about your
priorities (STEP 9)

=   The sum and substance of the information you need about yourself in preparation for choosing some future directions that will use these skills and accommodate your priorities.

RESOURCES

Defining Values

Simon, Sidney B., Leland W. Howe, Howard Kirschenbaum. *Values Clarification*. New York: Hart, 1972.

STEP 5: Listing Your Likes

List about a dozen things you like or like to do,
watch, or listen to. They may include things you
have liked in the past. (Forget about whether or
not you have any skill involved.) In the right
column try to state WHY you like them. Then list
some places you like and why.

          Things I like   Why I like them

_____   _____

_____   _____

_____   _____

_____   _____

_____   _____

_____   _____

_____   _____

_____   _____

_____   _____

_____   _____

_____   _____

_____   _____

_____   _____

     Places and Surroundings   Why I like them
            I like

_____   _____

_____   _____

_____   _____

_____   _____

STEP 6: Recording Your Wishes

* If you did not have any responsibilities or have to earn a living, how would you use your time? (Exclude complete idleness.)

  What appeals to you most about it?

* What courses would you like to take for fun?

* If you had $50,000 given you to use on something other than yourself or family, how would you spend it?

* If you were interviewed by your local newspaper 10 years from now, what would you like them to report about you?

* What do you think needs doing in the world?

  What would YOU actually want to do about it?

* Assuming there were no limitations on you, what would be your absolutely ideal, dream occupation?

  What especially appeals to you about it?

  The space provided is limited. You may want to use additional sheets.

STEP 7: Identifying Your Musts

    A. Review Experience #1 on your Transkills Chart
       and enter in the left column on the chart below
       the answer to this question:

       "WHAT GAVE ME SATISFACTION IN THIS EXPERIENCE?"

EXPERIENCES

SATISFACTIONS	#1	#2	#3	#4	#5	#6	#7	#8

       Answer the same question for each of the other
       experiences and check off any words that repeat;
       add new ones.

    B. List any other things that you value greatly or
       that are important to you (see instructions, page
       30). If you have trouble with this, go through
       your answers to all the WHY questions in STEPS
       5 and 6.

    C. Circle any of the satisfactions or values in A
       and B that are absolutely essential to you in
       the future. These are your MUSTS.

STEP 8: Selecting Your Special Knowledge Skills

Jot down any special knowledge, subject matter, or
know-how that you have and that you would like to
make use of in your future.

Below are listed some areas that might remind you
of such knowledge or know-how:

From school: _____

_____

_____

From other courses, seminars, or training: _____

_____

_____

_____

From paid work: _____

_____

From non-paid activities or service: _____

_____

_____

_____

From recreational activities: _____

_____

_____

From your "experiences" (STEP 1): _____

_____

_____

_____

STEP 9: Summarizing Your Priorities

From each of the previous steps, list the three
items most important to you:

From   Most Important Items

STEP 5:   _____
(Likes)
                     _____

                     _____

STEP 6:   _____
(Wishes)
                     _____

                     _____

STEP 7:   _____
(Musts)
                     _____

                     _____

STEP 8:   _____
(Special
Knowledge)   _____

                     _____

These "Most Important Items" are your Priorities.

4

Assessing Jobs For Transkills

You have now collected two kinds of information about yourself: your transkills (STEPS 1-4) and your priorities (STEPS 5-9). Your groupings of transkills constitute a person-description of yourself.

Your next moves are to learn and practise the method of assessing a job for its transkills (STEP 10), and then, in the next chapter, covering STEP 11, developing ideas for jobs that will use your transkills.

STEP 10: Assessing Jobs For Transkills

It would be simple if all you had to do was to match your transkills with the same kinds of words used to describe a job, that is, if your own person-description lined up with a job description. Unfortunately, employers do not usually describe their jobs in terms of transkills. They describe them in terms of duties or responsibilities. I shall call these "tasks."

All work, in fact all activity, is composed of tasks. If you play golf, two of the tasks are hitting the ball and keeping score. If you are a police officer some of the tasks are patrolling, making arrests, firing a pistol, testifying in court. These tasks require the specialized knowledge discussed in STEP 8 (p. 32, also p. iv). And this knowledge is not transferable to another occupation. Knowing how to fire a gun is not transferable to knowing how to play a harp. Obviously, such task descriptions do not fit you because you do not have the knowledge-based skills to perform them.

But these same tasks do require transkills, as well. Each task has an array of them. What are some that a police officer uses firing a gun?

I would say eye, hand, and body control; keeping cool; being accurate.

Having converted tasks into transkills, you will be in a position to see to what extent the transkills required by the job match your own. For instance, Terry reported none of the above transkills.

GROUP EXERCISE

There follows a picture of a well-known job, lines repair-person. I have suggested two tasks she performs. You can add two more tasks she does after the line is repaired. In the right column, jot down the transkills she uses for each task.

THE JOB

TASKS   TRANSKILLS

Get equipment ready

Repair line

An easy way to start analyzing a job for its tasks is to ask yourself three questions —

What do you do to get ready?

What are the main features of the job — the essence?

What do you do to wrap it up or close it out?

Take a life insurance salesman. Enter the tasks and transkills.

THE JOB

TASKS   TRANSKILLS

Incidentally, what would be some of the knowledge-based skills you'd need to sell insurance policies? Don't bother to write them down.

You need to learn about the different kind of policies and their costs.

And knowledge of the competition, too. But at this stage we don't need to worry about these knowledge skills.

As you start using this technique you should ask yourself three questions —

#1. What transkills are involved?

#2. Which transkills do you have? Make a mental note of these from STEP 4, i.e., your transkill grouping cards (p. 24).

#3. What is your gut reaction to this kind of work? Do you like or dislike it? If you feel neutral, you may get some clues by checking your summary of priorities in STEP 9 (p. 39).

People usually use three ways to assess jobs — observing, reading, and asking others. As you try out each way ask yourself the same three questions above.

Observing

Keep on the lookout for jobs and tasks that are around you every day — clerk in the drug store, detective on TV, politician in news photo. Here. I'll switch on TV to the news: weather commentator. His principal task is to tell us the forecast. Terry, what transkills is he using right now on the air, i.e., Question #1?

```
STEP 10: Assessing Jobs for Transkills

                        THE JOB

              Weather Forecaster

   Tasks                        Transkills

Preparing data          Researching, writing
                        Making calculations
                        Numbers

Announcing forecast     Presenting, Performing
                        Good with words
                        Explaining

Maintaining historical file   Record keeping, details
```

Well, he's got to be high on presenting and performing and explaining. That's his role with people when he's on the air. He's got to be good with words and be able to speak them forcefully.

Any others?

Probably some of the research work and writing. Also making calculations.

Question #2, do you see any other of your talents or transkills in that job?

Sure. I'm looking at my groupings cards from STEP 4 — numbers, details, record-keeping, explaining.

And Question #3, how do you feel about the job, your gut feeling?

It's got plenty of status and recognition. I'd like that, but I can't say it turns me on much. Somehow the weather seems a little impersonal.

That's what I mean by practising assessing jobs. You spot the transkills needed. You name those that relate to you. You indicate your feelings and preference. Nobody's trying to imply that you should or should not be a weather forecaster. It's just practice.

There are your examples of observing. When you go to the bank next time, observe what the teller is doing and what transkills it takes. You know: *accuracy, quick reactions, serving people, handling money, record keeping, handling data, observing.*

Reading

Looking up information in books, magazines, and newspapers is another common way to practise. You'll find now that you can read about a job and understand what it takes to perform it. You can read even the dullest descriptions and call the transkills. Take this one from the *Occupational Outlook Handbook*[1] and fill in the transkills that have been omitted.

TASKS	TRANSKILLS
First, the programmer decides what company records contain the information needed to prepare the documents. Next he makes a flow chart or diagram showing the computer what order to follow in doing each step. From the flow chart, the programmer writes detailed instructions telling the machine exactly what to do with each piece of information. He also prepares an instruction sheet for the computer operator to follow when the program is run.	*Investigating* *Handling data* *Visualizing* *Organizing*

Plus planning, problem-solving, giving instructions, writing. Hey, I have 'em all. But I sure wouldn't pass the gut test. I don't think I'd like it at all.

Can you figure why not?

I guess it lacks some of the things I like — interaction with people, being of personal service to them, moving around.

No need to comment. I wasn't suggesting that as a career for you. You're still just practising.

With this new approach you can read about any person's work and begin to understand it, because you are using the same terminology that you used in analyzing your own talents. Now you're reading about it in your own language. Next time you spot an article, "A Day in the Life of a Wheat Farmer," go through it this way. Even though you've never seen a wheat farm you'll have a pretty good idea of what transkills the farmer needs.

Asking Others

Some people like to gather information by talking to others. Hearing what people actually do during the day is a good way to find out what a career consists of. And you can get that information by asking them just that.

Here's a tape I've used over and over in this workshop.[2] The participants never fail to come up with this extraordinary array of talents with no trouble at all even though they've never seen a machine shop. There are a dozen transkills missing from the list. See if you can write them in.

TASKS	TRANSKILLS

My job is to run the machine shop in a
plastics manufacturing plant in a small
plastics town. We make the dies (or molds)
for simple toys. The molds are later inserted
into the molding machines that turn out
thousands of any particular item.

My job, that is, foreman of all the   *Supervising*
machinists and tool and die makers, is pretty
demanding; lots of pressure. I enjoy that.
Each day has its own crises, but it pretty
much follows the same routines.

We open at 7:30; I check absentees. Then I   *Inspecting*
give my group leaders any new assignments   *Setting goals*
and deadlines. We meet 'em, too.   *Meeting goals*

By 10:30 I'm ready to prioritize the new   *Reading   Evaluating*
orders that came in. Then I go up to
engineering to show 'em why a particular
blueprint won't work. We haggle over it but   *Negotiating*
after a while work it out. Another place I'm
always arguing with is the molding room.
Sometimes they claim our dies won't fit their
machines!

After the break I get the gang together and   *Speaking*
let them know what's happening, and listen   *Communicating*
to their squawks.   *Being sensitive*

In the afternoon it takes about an hour to
handle the paper work — make out accident   *Handling data*
reports, check payrolls, make estimates, sign   *Costing*
requisitions, et cetera.
That's pretty much the story.

*I can see quite a few of my talents in that interview. As a
matter of fact, every single talent I placed on my cards are
qualifications on that job! But I see some are missing, too.
All those about ordering people around.*

How do you like the sound of the place?

*I guess I'd have to see it first. But I'm not too keen on the
factory kind of situation. Just a feeling.*

That's a good example of how your interview might go.
Remember to ask the person what transkills *they* think they use.
Incidentally, did that story the foreman told remind you of
anything we've done in this workshop?

115739

Yes. Telling our own stories about our experiences.

Exactly the same process.

Before we meet again, get some practice in this art of transkills identification. Ask a parent, sibling, neighbor, teacher, postman, friend what they do during the day. Don't overlook the housewife or househusband. If you're embarrassed to ask people, tell them you're taking a course that requires field study. Then fill out your STEP 10 form (following). You can report your progress at the beginning of the next session.

After you've had some practice identifying transkills on jobs and assessing your feeling about them, then you're ready for the next move — developing your idea list of career directions (STEP 11).

FOOTNOTES

1. U.S. Department of Labor, Bureau of Statistics, *Occupational Outlook Handbook* (Washington, D.C. 1974), p. 109.
2. See Joseph L. Norton, *On the Job* (Chicago: Ferguson, 1970) for work diaries on 65 different jobs.

STEP 10: Assessing Jobs for Transkills

THE JOB

Tasks   Transkills

5

Developing Ideas For Exploration

This phase involves you for the first time in thinking about where to put your talents to use. So far your self-search has resulted in an inventory of your transkills, likes, wishes, musts, special knowledge and priorities. You are now ready to take this information about yourself and look around to see what kind of directions you can link it up to.

The intent of STEP 11 is to prevent you from rushing into a final decision. The aim is to help you generate a lot of ideas about jobs or careers that use your transkills.

STEP 11: Listing Ideas To Explore

I seldom find a person at this stage of the *Searchway* who hits on a terrific idea for a career direction and instantly adopts it for a goal. Picking careers just doesn't happen that way. The lightning does not suddenly strike as a reward for having done all this interior search work. You have to keep plugging away at the process.

So the next phase is not to seize on just one direction and start tracking it down. That might be easiest to do, but it gives you no alternatives. It only results in disappointment if your search leads nowhere.

Instead you need to build a list of just as many ideas for career directions as possible. From it you will choose one or two ideas that seem the most interesting to you and which you really feel are worth looking into. So this list is *not* one from which you necessarily choose an ultimate direction, but one from which you choose some directions to explore.

The list does not have to include just those directions that are realistic. Forget the realities for a moment.

I like the idea of a list, but I don't see the point of including the impossible. What good is there in listing something I'm just not qualified for?

Because from what you call an "unrealistic" career you may get an idea for a more realistic one. For instance, you might come up with transferable skills in *coaching* and *supervising*, plus a liking for young people and the outdoors. An ideal career direction obviously might be running a camp. This seems unrealistic to you, though, because you don't have the capital. But the notion of running a camp might spin off into being an assistant director of a camp or working with young people in a youth detention center.

There are five sources from which you'll probably draw these ideas:

Reviewing the principal transkills listed on your groupings cards (STEP 4).

Reviewing the likes, wishes, musts, special knowledge, and priorities you have listed in STEPS 5 to 9.

Observing jobs you see around you every day.

Reading about jobs, occupations, careers.

Asking other people's opinions.

Let's start with —

Reviewing Transkills

Look at your groupings cards (page 24) and see if you can associate any particular career directions or occupations with the transkills. For instance, a person who had groupings indicating *using hands, being artistic,* and *getting end results* might jot down some craft like carpentry or photography. In other words, you're converting your generic transkills back into some specific activities.

Reviewing Likes, Wishes, etc.

Review the material you developed in STEPS 5 to 9 (pages 35-39). Note those that you marked [F] for FUTURE. If you reported liking books, and had *attention to detail* and *organizing* as talents, you might jot down the idea of librarian. Or if you've got outdoors and mountain climbing under your STEP 5 "likes," don't be hesitant to put down a Himalayan mountain climbing expedition if that appeals to you. But for the time being keep your list to yourself. It's your private homework.

So if I love skating and also have some business sense for dollars, I should start up a skating rink?

No, I don't mean that you should or even would. All you're saying now is that running a skating rink is a possible idea to explore.

I'm sure you think this is way out. It is. And the reason is that in order to find yourself a career direction that suits your skills and likes, you're going to have to think imaginatively about it. This thing you're looking for is not going to automatically appear somewhere already neatly linked to you. You can't count on getting it off a computer print-out. This list is to start you thinking about yourself creatively. Probably some of these ideas will not hold too much interest for you. At this stage don't worry whether they do or not. We're looking for quantity of ideas. The more you can generate, the more spin-offs there will be.

Observing

As you walk or drive around, take note of occupations you see and what might lie back of them. Police officer calls to mind the court system, prisons, correctional work, crime in the streets. Are there any ideas there for you? As you drive by a travel agency ask yourself what jobs they need to help you to plan your next trip. Are there any occupations you see on TV that look interesting?

What about private eye?

I've found a number of people intrigued with that one. They don't actually want a job gum-shoeing on a city police force, but they like the idea of solving a riddle . . . TV is always interviewing different types — politicians, teachers, managers, bureaucrats. Do some ring more of a bell with you than others? If so, jot down the bell-ringers.

Reading

Some people don't read much, especially on this subject; but this stage merely involves skimming through lists for ideas.

Yellow pages: Flip through the yellow pages of the phone book and quickly note the businesses, employers, activities, and institutions that look more interesting to you than others.

Classified ads: Skim through the Sunday classifieds and list those of interest. You must absolutely ignore the education and experience requirements or you'll get discouraged. All we want now are ideas that trigger other ideas.

Reference books: In the library you should be able to find two publications of the U.S. Department of Labor:

Guide for Occupational Exploration, 1979. Run through the "Summary List of Interest Areas, Work Groups, and Subgroups," pages 9 to 12. If your library doesn't have it, ask them to order it.

Dictionary of Occupational Titles, 1977. Review the "Summary Listing of Occupational Categories, Divisions, and Groups," pages xxxiv to xli.

Go through this kind of material quickly for ideas. Don't stop to worry about whether your selections are realistic or whether you are qualified. Jot your ideas down on the form below, "STEP 11: Listing Ideas to Explore" (p. 60).

Asking Other People's Opinions

Show your friends, spouse, partner your groupings cards. Describe briefly what they mean to you. Ask them what kind of occupations a person with these skills is suited for. Ask them to think big and not allow their knowledge of you to limit their suggestions.

But I would think this would happen anyway. How can you prevent them from thinking about you the way they know you?

Because you are describing your transkills to them in a way which they have never thought about. You are asking them what occupation a person with these skills could investigate. Be sure not to tell them at first what your 10 experiences were. If you do, they'll tend to suggest things related only to the experiences. They won't think big enough. Add their ideas to your STEP 11 form.

Another way to get others' ideas is called "brainstorming." You may want to invite someone else in for this. But let's try it right now.

First, Terry copies the transkills from the revised STEP 4 groupings on a large piece of newsprint or easel paper and tapes it on the wall.

Second, tell us what this diagram means in terms of your principal talent areas.

TRANSKILLS GROUPINGS

Learning new
Studying up

Having ideas- Planning
Starting Things
Follow through w. details
Solving problems

Persuading
Promoting
Explaining

Handling money
Economizing
Keeping records
Numbers

Helping others
Cooperating (groups)

Communicating
Socializing
Contacting

I seem to use and enjoy a lot of transkills that have to do with thinking up new ideas, collecting information, explaining it to others, and influencing them. Then I put the ideas into action and carry through until I get results. I'm also pretty good at handling budgets and money.

All right. We'll build our ideas on those transkills. Let's go on. Third, write on another sheet of newsprint or easel paper —

IDEAS TO EXPLORE
FROM BRAINSTORMING

Fourth, the rest of us suggest careers, jobs, or activities that will use most of the transkills listed on the diagram. Terry writes them on the blank sheet as we suggest them. This is the brainstorming part. The six rules of brainstorming[1] are —

1) Throw in lots of ideas, thick and fast, the more the merrier.

2) Suggest things that seem way out regardless of whether you think Terry would like them or not.

3) Build on other people's ideas. I suggest forester, someone else suggests game warden. If you can't think of the name of the job, just say the area, like gardening, statistical work, health care.

4) Don't say anything negative about another's suggestion.

5) Don't go into why you made your suggestion or try to sell it. It takes too much time.

6) Terry, don't let on whether you like an idea or not. Keep a poker face. Why? Because if you scowl when someone suggests something you don't like, that may discourage us from suggesting anything more in that area.

Let's go. We've only got 15 minutes. Here are the suggestions we make and Terry writes them in.

IDEAS TO EXPLORE
FROM BRAINSTORMING

Social worker
Teacher
Community programs
Employment interviewer
Training in industry
City planner
Data processing
Treasurer of social agency
Fund raising
Administrator, Health/Welfare Dept.
Politics, campaign manager

Just one tip on brainstorming. There are many occupations and jobs that cut across the five main areas of work. These five are —

Private enterprise — business, industry.

Government — local, state, Federal, and military.

Education — schools, colleges, and universities.

Private non-profit organizations — social agencies, hospitals, associations, chambers of commerce.

Self-employment.

For instance, different forms of teaching and training are done in all five sectors. Personnel work exists in the civil service, publishing houses, and universities. Lots of careers you can enter by starting your own business.

*   *   *   *   *

As long as we've been working on this for 10 minutes, let's ask Terry for some clues that might help us focus in more. Terry, back in STEP 9 you summarized the most important of your likes, wishes, musts, and special knowledge skills. It would help us narrow our brainstorming if you would share some of these with us.

Well, out of the likes list I chose traveling, seeing new things, and I guess you'd call it encountering new kinds of people. (STEP 5)

That helps. What about some of your wishes and dreams? (STEP 6)

I'd like to be an author writing on the environment. Once in a while I think it would be nice to go into politics.

You're giving us plenty of clues, all right. Now for your musts. (STEP 7)

Two of them seem to be moving around and good pay.

Finally, what special knowledge skills are really important for you to make use of? (STEP 8)

I'd say I'd like to put to use what I know of environmental matters. The course I took in international relations; I'd like to learn more about it. I think I'd like to learn another language well.

Terry has given us a lot of new leads. We're finding out more about what kinds of interests and environments Terry likes. Sheer personal preference is most important in making a choice. None of us can judge that. Terry has to. Let's go again —

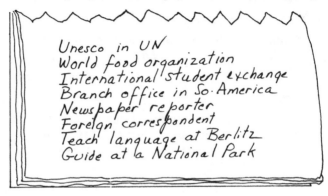

That gives you an idea of the kind of ideas for exploration you can pick up from others through brainstorming. Now, Terry, just check off those that appeal to you and that you might consider exploring.

I'll check city planning, politician, campaign manager, UN, international student exchange, pollster.

Now that we've completed brainstorming, can you tell us of any specific ideas you got on your own from STEPS 5 to 9 and from observing and reading?

Yes, from the "Things and places I like," I thought of San Francisco and realized in asking "why?" that I like cosmopolitan surroundings. Then the idea of meeting people made me think of running conventions in a big city (STEP 5).

I like the idea of a traveling fellowship studying people (STEP 6). That ties in with being a sociologist, I guess.

My dream job of running for office has to mean the occupation of politician. I guess the "Why?" is serving people . . . Maybe it would be fun to be an ambassador. But that's impossible.

Don't say "impossible." That's not the point just now. When you say "ambassador" you're naming a specific job, and the U.S. has only about 120. But much more important, what does that term itself suggest? What's connected with "ambassador?"

Everything to do with embassies, consulates, passports, negotiations.

I think you'll find that whole area of work is referred to as foreign service, isn't it? And there are undoubtedly a variety of jobs in the foreign service, besides the top one, ambassador.

Yes, I can think of one. The greeter person. What's that called?

Protocol chief? . . . Let's make sure, then, that you have the general area of work in mind as well as the specific job title.

JOB TITLE	AREA OF WORK
Convention manager	Convention management
Social worker	Social agency work
Teacher	Education
Employment interviewer	Personnel work
Campaign manager	Working in political campaign
Pollster	Public opinion surveying
Bank officer	Banking
Ambassador	Foreign service
Sociologist	Sociological research

Now you have an idea list in terms of both specific jobs and general career directions. That will broaden your options.

GROUP EXERCISE

Each person now takes his or her turn in going through the same process of brainstorming that Terry just completed. If there are too many of you to complete all the brainstorming in one session, you may have to carry it over to another.

* * * * *

As each of you completes the brainstorming you will need to know at once what to do next with this information. That is explained in STEP 12, "Sampling Career Directions," in the following chapter. In this way some of you will be able to carry out the next homework assignment right away.

FOOTNOTES

1. Alex F. Osborn, *Applied Imagination* (New York: Charles Scribner's Sons, 1963), p. 156.

STEP 11: Listing Ideas to Explore

6

Sampling Career Directions

As you each complete your brainstorming and compiling of a list of ideas, you must decide on two directions you want to take samples of. The point of a sample is to try something out to see if you like it without committing yourself to it. You don't have to buy it yet.

This sampling, though, is not a matter of someone handing you a small package to nibble on free of charge. It requires some work on your part because you actually have to get out and *act* on some of the decisions you've been making on paper and in conversation. There is no way around the next steps if you want to learn how —

— to firm up ideas for your directions,
— to find out about them,
— to test them out.

STEP 12: Sampling Career Directions

From your brainstorming list and your STEP 11 idea list (page 60) select two different career directions that appeal to you most. The next absolutely essential step is to investigate these personally. You simply cannot make an informed decision without investigating first-hand what this particular career direction consists of and whether it would suit you. No one else can do this for you. Here are the basic moves you'll have to make, although you may want to change the order or emphasis:

1) Ask everyone you can think of if they know anyone in the career field that you want to investigate. These personal

references are best. You'll be surprised how many names you'll collect.

2) Go through the Yellow Pages of the telephone directory to find names of employers connected with this career direction.

3) Go through directories in the library for such employers. Always remember there can be five kinds:

Government
Private enterprise
Non-profit organization
Educational organization
Self

Many occupations are found in all five.

4) Call or write at least two people in the areas of your choice. The higher up in the organization the person is, the better. The person may be a stranger or someone you know. Tell them that you are considering going into their kind of work and would like information about it. *Explain that you do not expect them to have a job and you will not ask for one.* Don't be bashful about your request; people like to talk about their fields and to give advice.

5) At the interview:

Always ask the person you're interviewing what tran-skills are required in the field and how he or she got into it. Don't let them get away with describing only the knowledge-based skills required.

Use the opportunity to describe which of these skills you think you have and why you are interested. This gives you more practice in relating your talents to the job. It also begins to rehearse you in explaining your own assets to others.

Assess your own gut feeling about the activity you are discussing and why you do or do not like it.

Ask your interviewee whether he or she can refer you to someone else in the field for a similar talk.

Don't be tempted to ask for a job. Remember you got this interview on the basis that you would not ask. If your person thinks you are going to pop the question, he or she will be more guarded in conversation. Your relationship will be applicant-employer instead of person-person. As this individual seldom has the authority to say "Yes" without consulting others, you're forcing a "No" just when he or she would like to be helpful.

After you leave, make some notes on your interview and add them to any other information you may have collected.

Write a thank-you note. This serves as a reminder of your visit.

YOUR HOMEWORK

Each of you has now decided on two career directions to explore through an interview. The next meeting date should allow enough time to arrange and complete the interviews. Come back ready to report your findings.

* * * * *

STEP 12: Sampling Career Directions (continued)

At this session we're going to hear what success you had interviewing someone for information. Terry?

I was interested in following up that idea of working with a group that handles foreign student exchanges.

I was talking to a friend about it. In fact, I showed him my skill groupings and he said he knew a Mrs. Vogel who has been working in something called North American Student Exchange. They arrange for students to come here and stay with a family, and vice versa.

I called Mrs. Vogel and made an appointment. Incidentally, later she told me she was glad I said I wouldn't ask about jobs because she hates to interview people looking for a job when she doesn't have any! She told me how she got into this work, and gave me a couple of names to follow up.

Then she described the work: they make contacts with all kinds of schools and agencies in Europe mostly, send out information and application blanks about the program, occasionally make trips abroad, talk to sources who know the applicants, hold endless meetings to decide among them, write and phone families all over North America to ask them to take students, make arrangements. I gather it gets pretty hectic as deadlines approach. Then there's all the business of looking into schools and what credit they'll get. It really sounds interesting. Some of the skills she thought she had were organizing, persuading people, and taking care of lots of details.

GROUP EXERCISE

Each of you should now tell about your own interviews and what your significant findings are.

* * * * *

This narrative story about your interview is really not enough to help you make a decision about whether or not you want to continue investigating this line of work. Inasmuch as this is a field you are not too familiar with, you need further analysis to determine to what extent your transkills already qualify you for it.

The two-page STEP 12 form that follows is designed to help you see how ready you are for this career direction, and, if you want to pursue it, what you would have to do to prepare yourself.

The best way to explain this STEP 12 form is for Terry and me to run through it together while Terry is filling it in. (See Terry's STEP 12 form that follows yours.) Terry, will you sample the job you just explored?

But I haven't really decided on this foreign student thing yet.

No harm. We're only sampling. But there's more to sampling than saying "go" or "no go." You can use it as a chance to weigh pluses and minuses. In doing this you may get notions of related career directions. Let's make a stab at this and not try to complete every question. Whenever we leave off, we'll indicate it with a row of dots (. . .).

First write in a career direction. Include those job duties for which you feel pretty sure you already have the talents, i.e. transkills. Avoid naming a job title; just name the main tasks you want to be performing. Add the kind of organization in which you want to be performing this work. See [1] on your form.

Now, from what you know about this career direction, list those qualifications which it requires and which are also your principal talents [2]. These will be the transkills on your grouping cards (STEP 4, page 55).

Probably being able to get things done would be important when you have to make arrangements to place a student in a school and home.

STEP 12: Sampling Career Directions (page 1)

Career Direction:

Qualifications:

STEP 12: <u>Sampling Career Directions</u> (page 2)

Special Knowledge or Know-how:	
Things the career direction requires but that I lack or have questions about:	Actions I could take to overcome these lacks:
Things that I require but the career direction lacks, or other reservations I have:	Comments:

STEP 12: Sampling Career Directions (page 1)

[1] Career Direction: *A position involving recruiting, interviewing, administration, follow-up for foreign student exchange program run by a university, government agency, United Nations, or private group.*

Qualifications:

[2] *Ability to get Things done on time; overcoming obstacles:*
[3]   *A. Planning bicycle trips for groups; Solving unexpected problems like running out of money, making repairs.*
    B. Starting up new employee orientation; interviewing, explaining rules...

[2] *Influencing other people:*
[3]   *C. Persuading classmate to study for exam.*
    D. Convincing employer to hire me.
    E. Getting church fair to keep prices low.

[2] *Maintaining records, attention to detail:*
[3]   *F. Writing reports/keeping accounts for environmental committee.*
    G. Collecting, recording money at fair.
    H. Scheduling and logging employees for orientation.

Now list the evidence that proves you have this ability [3].
Draw from your "experiences" in STEP 1. Have your verbs end
in "-ing." It conveys the sense that your skill is a continuing one,
not just something you did once in the past. Take another talent
that's essential to this job.

> *I can see how I'd have to be able to persuade American
> families to take the students in.*

These two transkills cover three of the duties you mentioned
above under the career direction you wanted, i.e. recruiting,
interviewing, and follow-up. What about "administration." What
does that mean?

> *Correspondence, phone calls, application forms is what
> Mrs. Vogel mentioned. That's a lot of detail.*

There's the summary of three key talents you already have
for this job, and the proof that you use them. That's what makes
them "qualifications."

> *Yes, but the job requires some other things I don't have.*

Maybe so. We'll tackle that problem in a few minutes.

Next come those qualifications, if any, that bear directly on
the career direction. They are usually based on some kind of
knowledge, know-how, or subject matter [4]. They are the special
knowledge skills you jotted down in STEP 8 (page 32). They
should tie in with foreign student exchange work.

> *One was my course in international relations; another my
> interest in reading about international events and politics.*

OK. But elaborate on them; give 'em some punch! . . .

This is the point where you ask yourself a tougher question:
What things does student exchange work require that you lack?
[5]

> *I don't see how I'm qualified because I really don't have
> any kind of experience.*

That's right. And you'll be up against people who may have.
How could you go about getting some kind of experience or
exposure?

> *Get connected with a family that has a student, I suppose.*

Also many non-profit agencies like this one have volunteer
programs. How could you find out about these? As you think up
these "actions you could take" to offset your lack of experience,
enter them in the right hand box under that heading . . .

STEP 12: Sampling Career Directions (page 2)

[4] Special Knowledge or Know-how: Received good mark in International Relations course in European cultures... Enjoy reading about foreign events, politics, investigating place names in atlases and encyclopedias...	

Things the career direction requires but that I lack or have questions about:	Actions I could take to overcome these lacks:
[5] I lack any experience.	Find family that is entertaining student. Look up local foreign student center. Volunteer my services; join hospitality committee.

Things that I require but the career direction lacks, or other reservations I have:	Comments:
[6] No travel involved. Is There status and recognition? Pay is on low side...	Maybe just meeting + corresponding with foreigners is ok for now. Don't know yet. Ask someone... Find out exactly. Also how much do I need?

Let's ask the reverse question: Is there anything you require that the career direction lacks or you have reservations about [6]? You may get some clues by reviewing your musts and priorities back in STEPS 7 and 9 (pages 31 and 33).

> *I said I wanted to move around and travel and that I liked recognition and status. Then pay is a priority matter, too.*

What do they pay?

> *I don't even know yet. I don't think they have much money. I'd better find out. Travel was what I thought of in connection with this work, but Mrs. Vogel says you don't really travel much.*

Your entries under "Action" and "Comments" are the moves you could make right away if you continue to be interested in pursuing this career direction. Usually they involve getting more information. And the more you get, the better informed you'll be for your ultimate decision.

For now put this worksheet on hold, and try out your other choice.

> *What's the point of two? Why isn't one enough for now?*

It's always a good idea to sample two career directions. Then you can make comparisons and see to what extent the transkills link up. What is your second sample, Terry?

> *Political campaigning. Here goes.*

Good. Name the activity rather than a job title [1]. Then you don't get locked in to a job they have that might be too far above you or too far below. If you want, name a few duties that you know the job calls for and you can already perform. These are the very same "tasks" which you learned to identify in STEP 10 (pp. 41-49)

And your qualifications for these duties [2]?

> *It looks as though I could use the same transkills I used for the foreign student exchange job. I'll add one: assisting people. And the evidence (indicated by A, B, C, D) is going to be mostly the same, too [3].*

If that's the case, just set them down in condensed form so we can see how they match up.

> *As a matter of fact, even the new transkill I added, assisting people, could be included with the foreign student exchange qualifications.*

It will always turn out that way. Because if you originally

STEP 12: Sampling Career Directions (page 1)

---

[1] **Career Direction:** Working in a political campaign headquarters, or for a public office holder, performing administrative duties, — taking calls, answering questions, expediting requests.

Qualifications:

[2] Ability to get Things done on time; overcoming obstacles:
[3]   A. Planning bike trips . . .
   B. Starting up employee orientation . . .

Influencing others:
   C. Persuading classmate . . .
   D. Convincing employer . . .
   E. Getting church fair prices set low . . .

Maintaining records, attention to detail:
   F. Writing reports . . .
   G. Collecting money . . .
   H. Scheduling employees . . .

Facility for assisting people who need help:
   I. Answering customers' inquiries at supermarket.
   J. Handling inquiries about environmental committee procedures.

develop your idea list in STEP 11 (page 60) on the basis of your transkills, then any career directions you select to look into are going to incorporate those same skills. Once you see how these core talents can work for you, you can explore and sample endless varieties of career directions that interest you. I think we can skip the rest of the form for now.

GROUP EXERCISE

Each of you should now begin developing the STEP 12 forms (pp. 65-66) for your two alternative career directions. You might start these in this session and compare notes about your description of the career directions [1]; what transkills you already have that qualify you [2]; what evidence you have of these transkills [3].

Also, try to think of anything you have done in your life that is directly connected with your objective and that you could mention under the heading, "Special Knowledge or Know-How" [4]. Or it may be an interest you have taken in the subject through reading, or associating with a certain person or group.

YOUR HOMEWORK

Complete the forms for both career directions. Develop another informational interview in the same career direction or in another one. Continue as long as you feel you need to explore.

RESOURCES

Information and Referral Interviews

Germann, Richard and Peter Arnold. *Bernard Haldane Associates' Job and Career Building.* New York: Harper & Row, 1980. Pp. 74-94.
Figler, Howard. *The Complete Job-Search Handbook.* New York: Holt, Rinehart and Winston, 1979. Pp. 143-153.
Irish, Richard K. *Go Hire Yourself an Employer.* Garden City, N.Y.: Doubleday Anchor, 1973. Pp. 42-48.

7

The End Product

Your STEP 12 worksheets are sample summaries of the investigation you've been conducting about yourself. You have uncovered your hidden skills — your transkills — and affirmed them in writing. You have documented them with hard facts about your accomplishments. You have found they did indeed provide clues to your future pursuits because you have linked them to at least two directions that make use of them. This linkage is substantial; it indicates that you are already partly qualified for these directions, something you might not have suspected when you started this inquiry.

But you have probably not arrived at an ideal *solution* in such a short time. You have been *practising* detective work, but not yet successfully performing it. As you continue to practise, you will become proficient enough to find solutions.

What next?

On the basis of these worksheets, you should be able to make a limited decision about each direction —

Shall I continue to investigate it? OR
Drop it? OR
Modify it?

For example, Terry, you could decide to —

Continue to look into the prospect of working in a political campaign headquarters, OR

Drop the idea entirely (realizing it is not an election year or the candidates bore you), OR

Modify the idea (e.g., investigate working on a campaign to raise funds for Sierra Club, which amounts to adding another entry to your list of ideas to explore, page 60).

If you choose to drop the direction, you don't need to feel at a loss. You simply refer back to that list of ideas and choose another career direction that you'd like to investigate.

So don't wait on it. The sooner you start another investigation the better. This is the way all decision-making is done; you are right at the heart of the process. And now that you know how to go about it, you can always act. Action on your part keeps up your momentum.

In closing this *Searchway* workshop, first a word to those of you who, like Terry, are about ready for the job search; and then a word for those of you who are not.

If you are ready to hunt for a job and write a resume, you can see that most everything in your STEP 12 worksheets (except your "lacks" or the job's "lacks") is grist for your resume. Your transkills and the evidence of them can be used repeatedly in different versions. A resume that emphasizes qualifications by means of transkills is sometimes called a "functional" resume because you are pushing your general functional qualifications, rather than those based on similar experience. Many employment interviewers feel uneasy reviewing a functional resume like this. They are used to resumes that present, in reverse chronological order, your directly related experience.

Therefore, even though you are short on such experience, make the most of it by including anything in your educational or personal history that bears on your job objective (see examples of Terry's "special knowledge or know-how" on page 68). Then you can support it with a section on the transkills that qualify you. But also include somewhere a brief chronology that gives the reader a quick view of your history.

As explained earlier, the *Searchway* does not cover job hunting techniques, such as collecting prospects, letter and resume writing, making contacts, interviewing, and negotiating for salary. These are well handled in a number of books. The titles and authors are listed under "Resources" at the end of this chapter. Look up at least two. Then you'll see that although their basic themes are alike, the authors may use different techniques. Obviously their pet methods have worked for them, but might or might not for you! Try to pick and choose among them and develop a system that suits your style best.

Some of you are not planning to job hunt yet. As I said in the introduction, this process can also be used by non-job and non-career seekers. It is helpful to a student going on to more education. It is basic for homemakers who plan to return to work some time in the distant future. Why? Because those completed STEP 12 worksheets can show you how you could be preparing now for the future.

After we wind up this workshop, you will want to see how other people have used the technique and philosophy at different stages of their lives. In Part II, Chapters 8 to 14, you will find examples of applying the *Searchway.* They will help you to put to work what you have learned.

In the meantime, go to it!

RESOURCES

Job Hunting

Billingsley, Edmond. *Career Planning and Job Hunting for Today's Student: The Non-job Interview Approach.* Santa Monica: Goodyear, 1978.

Bolles, Richard N. *What Color is Your Parachute.* Berkeley: Ten Speed Press, 1980. A "Bible" for first-time job hunters and career changers. It covers identifying skills and values; creating a career objective based on talents; searching inside the hidden job market; identifying and approaching the person who has hiring power.

Bolles, Richard N. and John C. Crystal. *Where Do I Go from Here with my Life?* New York: Seabury, 1974. An exhaustive "course" in the creative career search; explicit details of each step. Section on translating transferable skills into the language of the market place is especially useful.

Bolles, Richard N. *The Three Boxes of Life and How to Get Out of Them.* Berkeley: Ten Speed Press, 1978. Applies the *Parachute* principles to getting out of the three boxes of Education, Work, and Retirement and melding them over a lifetime. Thorough treatment of transferable skills.

Catalyst. *Resume Preparation Manual: A Step-by-Step Guide for Women.* New York: Catalyst, 1979.

Djeddah, Eli. *Moving Up: How to Get High Salaried Jobs.* Berkeley: Ten Speed Press, 1971. All aspects of the job search.

Figler, Howard. *PATH: A Career Workbook for Liberal Arts Students.* Cranston, R.I.: Carroll, 1975. Emphasizes creating one's own career from a self-analysis of values and skills in preparation for the resume and job interview.

Figler, Howard. *The Complete Job-Search Handbook*. New York: Holt, Rinehart and Winston, 1979. Stresses the 20 basic lifetime skills required to make a job search and how to put them to use; how to sell yourself without high pressure tactics.

Germann, Richard and Peter Arnold. *Bernard Haldane Associates' Job and Career Building*. New York: Harper & Row, 1980.

Haldane, Bernard. *How to Make a Habit of Success*. Washington, D.C.: Acropolis, 1975 (original edition, 1960). This is the seminal work. Haldane blended the traditional "abilities" and "interests" into "enjoyed achievements" and therein found the "factors of success," i.e. skills that could be transferred from career to career; developed the concept of.clustering skills; introduced the functional resume.

Haldane, Bernard. *Career Satisfaction and Success*. New York: Amacom, 1974. Applies the system of identifying motivated skills to employees who want to advance.

Haldane, Bernard, Jean Haldane, Lowell Martin. *Job Power Now*, Washington, D.C.: Acropolis, 1976. A job finding guide for young people, including the writing of "qualification briefs."

Irish, Richard K. *Go Hire Yourself an Employer*. Garden City, N.Y.: Doubleday Anchor, 1973. Total process; contrasts functional vs. obituary resumes.

Jackson, Tom and Davidyne Mayleas. *The Hidden Job Market: A System to Beat the System*. New York: Quadrangle, 1977. Thorough treatment of developing prospects.

Jackson, Tom. *Guerilla Tactics in the Job Market: A Practical Manual*. New York: Bantam, 1978. A less expensive adaptation of the above.

Kotter, John P., Victor A. Faux, Charles C. McArthur. *Self-Assessment and Career Development*. Englewood Cliffs, N.J.: Prentice-Hall, 1978. An extensive workbook/textbook for a course developed at Harvard Business School.

Lathrop, Richard. *Who's Hiring Who*. Berkeley: Ten Speed Press, 1977. Many examples of cover letters and resumes for those job hunting in the same field.

PART II
Applying the Searchway

This part of the book — Part II — describes how you who have gone through the *Searchway* might apply it at various stages of your life. You can apply it —

8

In the Family

The family setting is unique for exposing young people to the concepts of the *Searchway*. But there are built-in drawbacks because children are necessarily dependent on parents. Dependency can be a deterrent to children's thinking about their future. Why should they if their parents are thinking for them? For instance, some parents hold a vision of seeing their kids through college. That will be two to four years after they become "adults" at age 18 and can vote, drink, drive, strike, bear arms, or decide to marry or take a partner. The parents' understandable aim of helping the child get a degree and a good job and become truly independent is vitiated by this protracted period of dependency. Furthermore, the dependency factor in the early years is so potent it carries over to other institutions — school, college and employer. The array of other authority figures through life is formidable: baby sitters, day-care tenders, elementary and junior and high school teachers, counselors, principals, admissions officers, professors, deans, bosses, church and government personages. Dependency on them through life is a norm.

Of course, there are always rebel children whom this discussion need not concern. But most of us learn and respect the need to accommodate those on whom we are dependent. We are likely to have a habit of pleasing our superiors and "keeping in good" with them.

A woman who came to me for retirement counseling said that now she could finally start saving because she had just completed putting her two sons through graduate school at the University of Minnesota. She was proud of this because with degrees they could make it in the world. Later, one of her sons told me he never really wanted to go to grad school, but his mother wanted him to and financed it. So he did it to please her.

Pleasing others? Any harm? Certainly, if you have not learned how to assess your own desires versus your benefactor's.

A provocative aspect of dependency in the family is the role of the parent as chief evaluator. And parents cling to it. Quite normal. Their own parents trained them in the techniques, and they in turn practise them with a barrage of censure.

> "You're tired, you're staying out too late . . . You haven't studied much this week . . . Your hair's too long . . . You take too much time in the bathroom . . . You drive, eat, spend money too fast."

Gradually these evaluations are combined with sight-setting.

> "You really ought to take the college prep course . . . Engineering is a good field for someone with a talent in math like you . . . A security college is an absolute must."

As children get older parents may voice their appraisals less often and audibly. But the unvoiced critique is always present. There isn't a son or daughter who hasn't gathered or guessed what a parent wants him or her to be or be like.

> The day after Vice-President Calvin Coolidge was dramatically sworn in as president, his son, Calvin Jr., a student at Amherst College, showed up as usual at his summer job in a Connecticut Valley tobacco field. A co-worker remarked, "If my father was just made President, I wouldn't come in to work." Young Calvin replied, "If your father was my father you would."

Calvin Jr. read these Vermont vibes correctly. Children file their parents' unspoken goals in their memory bank for future reference. School counselors are constantly receiving such data: "My father thinks I should go to work." "My mother wants me to take a shorthand course."

Even when parents' input is outdated, the child may refer to it as gospel. "My parents never liked the idea of my going to ed school," Alice tells me on getting her MAT degree. Her info is two years old; she never checked it out to see if her parents still harbor that position.

These parental evaluations and recommendations, whether overt or covert, are difficult for children to cope with, because they simply do not know the appropriate presentations and rebuttals. If Jane knows what it is she wants to do, it may come across as a whim because she has no data to back it up. That's frustrating to her and her parents. And it is even more so when she does not know what it is she wants to do, but does not want to go along with her parents' pitch.

A high school grad tells me his father, a scientist, wants him to train for science or engineering. "He thinks if I really applied myself to math I could make it." The son accepts his father's interest in advising him, but simply does not know the words to explain why he can do, but does not like math, and why the scientist's life in a big organization sounds hemmed in. What's more, he can't counter this dislike with a declaration of his likes.

Obviously, this offspring needs exposure to the art of self-evaluation.

Seizing Opportunities

Here it is that the family, in spite of limitations put on it by dependency, offers a unique opportunity for teaching and training. No other authority will ever have it. Parents can learn and pose the questions that their children should be asking about themselves. Although these questions are like those in STEPS 1, 2, and 3 of the *Searchway*, it is not necessary to learn and teach it formally. In fact, the more informal the parent can be, the better. Kids associate formal teaching with the classroom which is just the setting to shun. The trick is to be ready with helping questions and to seize opportunities as they occur.

They occur when the child brings up any kind of pleasant experience he or she has had or wants to have. The best ones to pick are those that —

— are experiences of the moment raised by the child, often for the first time;

— concern matters about which the parent does not need to take a negative position or make a negative evaluation;

— are experiences that the child enjoys or thinks will be enjoyable.

"Hey, Mom, Sue said she'll teach me to ride her bike.". . . "They asked us if we wanted to visit the museum, so I signed up.". . . "I think I'll go out for the soccer team this year."

Let me address you now as the parent. Your response to such comments, inasmuch as you instantly decide you don't have to take a negative position, is to show your positive interest. "Fine," "Great" or "Good!" Then your child knows you're tuned in.

Your next move is to get the child to talk more about it. You will, of course, have your own approach that works, but the purpose of the conversation, however brief, is to start the child thinking about at least one of three aspects of an experience. If you have gone through the *Searchway* you are already familiar with them. Here are the three aspects to explore and examples —

ASPECT	EXAMPLE
When Jack/Jill has this experience, what does J/J actually do? What are the "tasks" involved? (Describing the experience, STEP 2, p. 6).	"What did Sue tell you is the first thing you do learning to ride a bike?"
What transkills does this experience make use of? (Identifying transkills, STEP 3, p. 11).	"When you play soccer for the first time, what is the main team skill you're going to need?"
What is the big satisfaction J/J gets out of it, leading to the "Why do it?" (Identifying satisfactions, STEP 7, p. 30)	"What's the biggest kick you got out of the museum trip?"

Getting your child to describe the experience (the first aspect above) may be the best starting point. In my workshops over the years, I find that young people will talk about a personal experience once they realize that it doesn't need to involve expertise and that someone is really interested in hearing about it. If you know nothing about a topic a child raises, you can show you want to learn about it. If you already know the ropes, you can ask how it's done differently from the way you learned.

The second aspect to explore — helping J/J to identify transkills — may not produce rapid responses. But you can always have in mind a few transkills to call attention to in a quick dialogue.

Learning to ride a bike: "When you get on to the bike, what's the main thing you have to do?" (That could produce the transkills of *keeping one's balance, body coordination, physical activity.*)

First soccer game: "Before the game, do you eat a heavy or light lunch? (These get-ready tasks always involve *planning.*)

Trip to museum: "I know this sounds like a stupid question, but when you are in the museum, what are you actually doing most of the time with your eyes?" (Obviously *observing*, and then, hopefully, *evaluating!*)

These examples sound simplistic. They are. You would naturally weave them into the dialogue as the openings arose.*

There is one transkill that you can not only help children become aware of, but also help them practise. That is *decision-making.* No one in the child's early life has more opportunity than you. *Decision-making* is a transkill used in every hour of the day awake. You do not need a course to learn or teach it.

Parent: How did you decide to go to the museum instead of band practice?

Child: *The science teacher said it's the only time she could arrange; so I asked the music teacher and he said to go ahead.*

P: That's good. You got some more information first before you decided. That's what you did the time I invited you to come into town with me. You talked to Joe first and decided not to. (Collecting all pertinent information is always the first move in making decisions.)

C: *I want to go to scout camp this summer. Al's going.*

P: Well, sounds good. Are there any other things you'd like to do?

C: *Earn some money.*

P: Do you want to make a list? Then you can decide which are the most important. (Considering alternatives is the next move in decision-making.)

By occasionally going through this routine you demonstrate that there is some sort of orderly process that facilitates decision-making. But beware! In the beginning pick up on things the child wants to do and about which you can remain at least mildly approving no matter which way the decision goes.

As you get practice on inconsequential doings, you can begin to use the method on those that do concern you and your opinions.

---

* The mood and occasions for such dialogues is described in the series on values clarification by Simon, Howe, Kirschenbaum and Olds. See "Resources" at end of chapter.

C: *Jack's going to drive us to the bowling alley.*

P: What do you think of the way he drives? You already know my opinion.

C: *I know, Dad, but he's getting better.*

P: Have you thought of any other ways of getting there?

By learning to explore alternatives to what appear at first to be single solutions, you may some day avoid blurting out, "Have you thought about what college you'd like to go to?" This loaded query assumes your child is going to college and neglects the possibility of an alternative. If you are afraid to raise the issue of an alternative because it might be grabbed at, relax. The child's basic position against going to college may sound like an unbudgeable, "I don't want to." But it could be a cover-up for any of these positions. "I don't want to —

— go to your college
— be a professional person
— study liberal arts subjects
— go for four years
— go next year
— spend your money on it.

After you have together weighed the pros and cons of college vs. work you may find ways to meet these objections, or find suitable alternative solutions. If the child remains firm about going to work, you have the chance to discuss some of the ideas in the *Searchway* about choosing a career.

The third aspect to explore is what satisfactions the child got or expects to get out of the experience. STEP 7 of the *Searchway* suggests that by considering the kicks we get out of experiences we begin to sense our own values.

C: *I beat Sarah today 7-5, 6-4.*

P: You're getting pretty good. What did you like most about that?

C: *Winning, of course!* (Or it could be something to do with improving, or showing others; or feeling good afterwards. Possible values: competition, achieving, status, self-development.)

Naturally, you may want to instill some of your own values, without being too preachy. Just pick a behavior of yours that illustrates that particular value and demonstrate it consistently in the child's presence, such as —

Driving safely by being law-abiding: when J/J is watching you drive, make sure the speedometer reading jibes with the posted speed signs.

Working for a living: try talking more about the good things that happen on your job than the bad.[1] Once in a while give a notion of the purpose of your work.

Just make sure that your own behavior relative to the value is reasonably consistent. What you or your child each *do* about your respective values carries more weight than what you each *say*.

In summary, you can apply the principles of the *Searchway* by encouraging your children to talk when they bring up experiences they have enjoyed or believe they will enjoy, and on which you do not have to take a negative position. Getting them to describe these experiences and to talk about the skills and values involved will heighten their awareness of these assets.

FOOTNOTES

1. Mangum, Garth L., G. Donald Gale, Mary L. Olsen, Elwood Peterson, Arden R. Thorum, *Your Child's Career: A Guide to Home-Based Career Education* (Salt Lake City: Olympus, 1977), p. 78.

RESOURCES

Decision Making

Gelatt, H.B., Barbara Varenhorst, Richard Carey. *Deciding.* New York: College Entrance Examination Board, 1971.

Gelatt, H.B., Barbara Varenhorst, Richard Carey, Gordon P. Miller. *Decision and Outcomes.* New York: College Entrance Examination Board, 1973.

Mangum, Garth L., G. Donald Gale, Mary L. Olsen, Elwood Peterson, Arden R. Thorum. *Your Child's Career: A Guide to Home-Based Career Education.* Salt Lake City: Olympus, 1977, pp. 177-186.

Values Clarification and Dialogues

Kirschenbaum, Howard, "Clarifying Values at the Family Table," *Readings in Values Clarification,* ed. H. Kirschenbaum and Sidney B. Simon. Minneapolis: Winston, 1974.

Simon, Sidney B., Leland W. Howe, Howard Kirschenbaum. *Values Clarification.* New York: Hart, 1972.

Simon, Sidney B. and Sally Wendkos Olds. *Helping Your Child Learn Right from Wrong.* New York: Simon & Schuster, 1976, Ch. 15, "Clarifying Responses," pp. 157-161.

9

At School

The school, like the family, has limitations as a place to encourage thinking freely about oneself. Authority figures abound — teachers, counselors, principals, coaches and custodians. Computers spew printouts of schedules; bells ring the 50-minute periods. Pupils are dependent on all of these 180 days a year for 12 years.

Evaluation, spontaneous in the family, goes formal in schools. Schools are perpetually measuring students' performance against that of others' or against norms. Schools test for grade placement level, research statistics, and college admissions. This torrent of assessment by others does not contribute to assessment by self.

Learning to self-assess calls for just the opposite environment. The prime topic, after all, is oneself. The authority and source of knowledge must be oneself.

This transition from being the recipient of evaluation to being the initiator is not easy. Faculty and staff will at times have to muzzle their ideas about what they think the pupil is or should be, and let him or her start making some judgments on this matter. They need to boost the student into this new role.

This chapter is aimed at those educators (and parents) who have the desire to see their young people take charge of this new on-going investigation about themselves.

Base Line: Experiences

The starting point for this research is, in current jargon, "where the person is at." The topic is not introduced by discussing careers, work values, and other such material. The kickoff is the topic the child is already immersed in and competent to talk about, that is, him or herself. The Fairfield, Connecticut, elementary schools handle it beautifully.

On the child's evaluation form there had been a section for a year-end comment. The instruction originally read: "Teacher will note one characteristic, talent, personal quality or accomplishment for which each child deserves individual recognition." A similar version now starts out: "Teacher and child in conference will identify one talent . . . etc."

Together they share the evaluation; together they find something from the child's history that was successful; together they make the first move towards self-understanding. Without having to refer to a manual, the Fairfield schools implemented the first tenets of career education. "The prime approach to self-understanding . . . is helping students see what they have accomplished," says Kenneth B. Hoyt, U.S. Director of Career Education.[1]

Skillspotting

A career education coordinator in a Fitchburg, Massachusetts, junior high school carried the process a little further. At the first session of her class each child wrote a story about something that he or she had done that was "great." Take Ruth. She described running every Monday afternoon in the physical fitness program and winning a race. Coordinator and class then pulled out what she called the "adjectives" — *outdoors, physical, winning, excited, worried, challenging, learning new, following orders, using muscles.* Ruth logged them on a chart that she made on a big piece of pink construction paper and checked them off under her first story.

Next week they drew pictures about something they'd enjoyed a lot. Ruth drew one of crocheting, and with the class, found the right adjectives and checked them on her chart — *using fingers, counting, using care.* In Week Three everyone described a fantasy. Ruth's was a trip to Florida. Some new adjectives were *moving, watching, buying.*

At the eighth session the coordinator showed an occupational film strip. An aircraft assembler was working on the wing of a DC-10 in the McDonnell-Douglas plant in St. Louis. Within 10 minutes the class had called out such traits as *physical activity, tense, well-organized, making money, planning, following orders, indoors, using hands, using a tool, making something.* They argued about *worrying,* whether or not he had to take care. They concluded, "Yes, he did. If he messed up, the plane might crash." And this was four years before the DC-10's pylons became notorious! The coordinator summed up what happens when children learn to identify their own adjectives: "Then the relationship between the adjectives about themselves and the adjectives describing the job becomes quite clear."[2]

I remember when I first discovered this phenomenon at Wayland High School. A group of seniors had completed writing up life experiences and identifying the transkills used. A kid challenged me, "Well, what do we do now with these things?" I groped for an answer. At that moment a landscape gardening truck bristling with rakes and shovels passed by. "Quick," I yelled, "factor out that landscape gardener's job!" From around the classroom came a bombardment —

> "Aesthetics . . . manual . . . outdoor . . . orderly . . .
> physical . . . manual operations . . .mechanical . . .
> taking care of . . . liking nature."

One boy who had already come up with some entrepreneurial talents of his own observed, "I think the guy's in business for himself." So what would that take?

> "Handling money . . . record-keeping . . .
> planning . . . customer relations . . . salesmanship . . .
> reliability . . . aggressiveness . . . buying."

These are overly dramatic examples of how quickly a young person can link up a fact about him/herself to the world of work. Beware! It may be merely an exercise in learning something new that day, like a new tennis stroke. Teachers of career education are aware of how few seeds may root. It's necessary to scatter the seeds a little further.

At Cathedral High School in the South End of Boston the teachers of the *Searchway* do not rely on just linking transkills to jobs to prove the point. They challenge students to find all kinds of activities in their daily lives where they use and enjoy these skills. Activities usually fall into three categories. Those outside school include babysitting, driving, playing instruments, shopping, dancing, making home repairs. Those inside school include the usual extracurricular activities. Lastly, activities as a "student" include taking notes, researching and writing papers, solving math and lab problems, studying textbooks, reciting lessons.[3] The intriguing thing about these requirements of the student is that they are obviously translatable into the transkills of *record-keeping, researching, writing, solving problems, studying-up,* and *presenting.* The skills required of any student of any subject are transkills.

Classes provide a chance to point this out. But always wait until a volunteer comments favorably about something learned.

Bernie said he liked the lesson on Abraham Lincoln. After he'd explained why he liked Lincoln, the teacher got him to name some other skills he'd used while gaining this information about the President. That involved *studying, making notes* and *explaining to others.* On this particular occasion he had shown all the earmarks of a real student. By making this self-analysis he was unboastfully giving himself due credit.

Two other transkills that are commonly used by the student are the skills of *analyzing* and *comparing.*

The teacher had written a list of birds on the board including "Barn swallow," and further down, "Song swarrow." A kid calls out, "What kind of a bird is a swarrow?" Someone else chimes in, "No, she means swallow." "No, sparrow." Instead of just correcting the spelling, the teacher asks them what they're doing when they find this blooper. They figure out it's *comparing* and then they concoct other examples where you use it, like shopping, filing, reading TV listings.

As for *analyzing,* that goes on whenever youngsters make plausible suggestions.[4]

Once they begin to see that transkills keep popping up in all kinds of situations, they can be shown the difference between transkills and the knowledge-based skills learned more formally. Social studies, Spanish, art, shop, music, computer languages are subject-matter that is not transferable between experiences that are different. Programming, a special field, is no use in talking to a Cuban refugee in Spanish. But programming makes heavy use of the skill of *logical reasoning* which is transferable through the widest range of mental activities.

These differences are important to teach. Though the field of computers may look fearsome to some, youngsters can relate themselves to it by asking to what extent they enjoy using logic to solve problems, e.g., in playing chess.

There are at least four skills that qualify both as knowledge-based and also transferable because they are learned both informally and formally. They are the old *Reading, Writing,* and *'Rithmetic,* plus what has always been implied, *Talking/Listening.* Everyone needs them to survive in our culture. Almost every basic activity demands them — driving, telephoning, cashing checks, and communicating essentials to the boss and the plumber.

The purpose of teaching the whole range of transkills in the classroom is to provide links that allow students to relate to appropriate jobs and occupations that exist all around them. The Department of Labor's new *Guide for Occupational Exploration* comments that there has been no way for a counselor to get information from a counselee in the same language as that used by employers in describing jobs.[5] Transkills provide that language.

The practical uses of this language in schools are numerous. Teachers and counselors no longer need to feel they first have to become experts about job content in order to teach the subject in the traditional way. Instead, they teach transkills identification as a basic approach, and then flash descriptions of jobs, as it were, and let students analyze them for the skills used. The DC-10 aircraft assembler and the landscape gardener, mentioned above, are examples. STEP 10 (pp. 41-47) provides examples of police officer, utility linesperson, insurance agent, weather forecaster, computer programmer, and machine shop foreman. Any group that has learned transkills identification can fathom these. Even more effective, of course, is to analyze a job which the student already has an inkling of.

Brainstorming

Another kind of exercise for a class that has learned transkills identification is brainstorming, described in STEP 11 (pp. 54-59).

Billy had a low level of self-esteem and had difficulty coming up with his life-experiences and transkills. When his turn for brainstorming came, though, he wrote on the board these groupings —
Investigative/scientific/technical
Detail/Record-keeping
Reading/Writing
Manual dexterity
Serving and helping people
Among the 20 suggestions from the class was dentist. Billy circled it. "Huh, never thought of that." More later on how Billy acted on this.

Payoffs

Mere exercises, though, do not hold attention. Career choice may not be the first order of business with a high schooler. Teachers and counselors report there needs to be immediate payoff. Here are some examples I have had contact with:

Resume Writing

An English teacher/advisor at The Winsor School in Boston used transkills identification with a unit in "Persuasion." The end-product was a resume for a summer job. Her summing up was this: "We felt the approach to be practical, effective and fun, to say nothing of revealing about one's skills and interests . . . Even more important was the way the students came to think about careers and about themselves as people."

The career education and placement counselor at Cathedral High School made the end-product a "job power report" a la Bernard Haldane.[6]

JOB POWER REPORT OF   Charlie Monell
                                    461 E. Brookline St.
                                    Boston 02118

My Skills Include: Able to communicate well with others, I apply knowledge well, I'm a good planner; also I persuade and direct others well. I am very much physically active and work well with a team.

Proof: Won senior class elections by campaigning and using knowledge to plan campaign. After being elected I got a lot of things going by getting others working for me. I am a member of my High School football team and execute well with them.

Interest: Included are all sports, chess, plus coin and stamp collecting.

College Applications

A high school senior was about to detour a question on a college application form about her activities; she could think of none. When challenged at the first session of a *Searchway* workshop, she suddenly struck on playing tennis and serving on the student council, and described them. Next class she said she had completed the application form with a story about each and the transkills she used.

At Vassar the admissions interviewer asked, "What adjective describes you best?" The candidate gulped, then recalled her talent areas. "Well, I guess I'm pretty good at helping people." Then she gave two examples.

A high school counselor reported that for the first time he had solid skills to mention in his letters of recommendation to colleges and the proof to back them up.

Work Explorations and Exposures

A group of students interviewed the administrator of the large equipment systems laboratory of Raytheon Company. Both he and the students had been primed not to spend time talking technicalities. When he tended to emphasize the product or process we would bring him back with a question like, "How did you get where you are?" or "What is it like?" or "What basic skills do you use in this work?" The result was that his talk was laced with phrases like, "make things happen," "get involved," "inquire about problems," "decide priorities," "make sure engineers are fully engaged," "develop engineers," "build up our library," "persuade the bosses to install automated drafting machines."

Afterwards one of the girls who had not peeped allowed, "I liked it; he talked about things I'm interested in — getting people to do things." Human relationships hold wide appeal.

A visit like this that stresses transferable skills will be more meaningful to visitors than one that harps on operations, sales volume, growth, and other measures of success. True, a few kids might latch on to one of these topics and learn something. But watch any plant tour. A minority are up front showing interest; the rest chatter, lag, or wait restlessly to be led to the next sideshow.[7]

Identifying skills plus brainstorming occupations can help students decide on their outside school projects or internships. Take Billy again, at the Buckingham, Browne & Nichols School in Cambridge. In the brainstorming session someone had suggested dentistry as a career. He liked the idea for his senior project. His father knew someone at Harvard Dental School. The dentist and Billy worked out a project at the Harvard Medical School's Animal Research Center taking cultures of primates' gums. At the end of the year Billy read his report to his class and showed some gory slides of a tooth being extracted from one of his patients, a baboon! His classmates and the dentist called out the transkills Billy used and we wrote them on an easel. Here is the list of Billy's tasks and the transkills used:

BILLY'S TASKS

Injecting patient
Using scalpel
Cutting tissue to 1/30 inch
Suturing
Taking samples
Using microscope
Taking photographs
Using lab run-
  through machines
Reading manuals
Assisting doctor

TRANSKILLS BILLY USED

Detail	Technical
Manual	Scientific
Dexterity	Persevering
Strong stomach	Recording
Patience	Organizing
Research	Writing
Reading	Memorizing
Taking	Team work
direction	Problem
Learning	solving
Analyzing	Curiosity

In spite of this revelation of Billy's skills, none of which even refer to dentistry, the questions from the floor were about the technology, the procedures, the species. They focused on the knowledge-based aspects of the project. I remarked on this to Peter Gunness, the headmaster. His insightful rejoinder was, "Well, that's what we teach 'em, don't we?"

However, Billy had a broader perspective. He wrote: "This experience made me realize I can do anything I put my mind to. Six months ago I never thought I'd have the skills necessary to do detail precision work needed on a lab project. I gained enough confidence in myself. I began to think more in analytical terms. Now I know I can stick to it."

Although the school counselor pegged this case as "smelling like a rose," it illustrates the power of using transkills to broaden people's views of themselves and their potentials.

Using the Part-Time Job As a Lab

The big payoff for knowing your transkills comes when it is time to find the first part-time job. All the principles discussed so far apply. They will be covered in detail in Chapter 11 on getting your first regular job. However, there is more to it than employment.

The first part-time job while at high school can be a unique training experience if teachers, counselors and student view it that way. Instead of seeing it merely as a stop-gap income-producer, a counselor/teacher can encourage students to report what is going on, what they like or dislike about it, and to what extent their talents are being used, just as Billy did. In chats with a group of work-study kids, for instance, a counselor/teacher can recycle some of the questions to ask when assessing jobs (STEP 10, page 44) — "What skills are required?" "Which do I have?" "What's my gut feeling about this place?"

A counselor can also make sure students in a work/study group assess to what extent they are successfully employing their four basic survival skills — *reading, writing, arithmetic,* and *listening/talking.* The group can provide its own first-hand examples of how critical these basic competencies are on the job —

"We have to read the instruction board every morning, or else.". . .

"You have to check your paycheck at once, or they'll give you a hard time changing it."

"If my machine conks out, the boss says to report it quick."

"I have to leave a note for the night shift about what's left to do."

If a student is having trouble with these communication and calculation transkills, there's no harm pointing out that they are all taught at school and there's still time to improve them.

There are four other transkills students can compare notes on and decide how well they're applying them. These are *taking direction, taking responsibility for a task, adapting to* and *cooperating with others.* They are all listed on the Transkills Finder in STEP 3, page 13. They are all used at school and are crucial on the first days, weeks, months on the new job. Although not listed in the formal job requirements, they are what the boss is really looking for. The know-how based skills (e.g., labelling a package, pushing a wheelchair, making out vouchers) are easy enough for the boss to teach and the new employee to learn; but the boss doesn't have time or patience to teach the transkills. A counselor and group, though, can discover their relevancy.

At Cathedral High one rap session is devoted to two questions: "What do you look for in a boss?" and a list is developed on the board. Then the reverse question is posed, "What traits do you think the boss looks for in you?" and a parallel list drawn up. The lesson, of course, is that the lists look alike. For instance, *keeping promises* on the boss's part resembles *fulfilling assignments* on the employee's part; *giving orders clearly* is like *speaking up clearly. Listening* is in order for both parties.

This use of the part-time job as a free training lab is a natural for schools interested in implementing the ideas of career education. The lab is there ready and waiting to be used with pay! All the school needs to do is to get the students who use the lab to talk about their experiences there. The linking of education and work, which everyone for years has talked about, is at hand!

FOOTNOTES

1. Kenneth B. Hoyt, "Career Education: Challenge for Counselors," *Vocational Guidance Quarterly*, June 1975, p. 306.
2. Dania Jekel, "An Integrated Career Education Program at an I.G.E. School," unpublished report prepared for the McKay Campus School, Fitchburg, Mass., November 1976.
3. Harold L. Munson, "Career Education Reconsidered: A Life-Experiences Model," *Personnel & Guidance Journal*, November 1978, pp. 136-139.
4. Garth L. Mangum, J.W. Becker, Garn Coombs, Patricia Marshall, *Career Education in the Academic Classroom* (Salt Lake City: Olympus, 1975), p. 84.
5. U.S. Department of Labor, Employment & Training Administration. *Guide for Occupational Exploration* (Washington, D.C., 1979), p. 323.
6. Bernard Haldane, Jean Haldane, Lowell Martin, *Job Power Now!* (Washington, D.C.: Acropolis, 1976) pp. 41-66.
7. Henry G. Pearson, "'Person Skills' vs. Job Techniques — An Answer to Student Orientation," *Personnel Journal*, May 1978, pp. 247-249.

10

At College

College offers you a unique opportunity — a two- to four-year period devoted to continuous learning. Such an intensive stretch of learning does not exist for adults elsewhere. Neither the home nor the job can provide it. It's the specialty of the college environment.

People generally do not understand what it is you are learning that is of real significance. They think of you as majoring in science, history, economics, journalism, or nutrition — all certified by a degree. They see you as a student of these subjects and assume your purpose is to become knowledgeable about them. You probably think the same.

Though you are partly right, that is a limited view of what you're getting for an investment of several years of your time and thousands of your dollars.

Your return on your investment does not eventually pay just because you took 25 courses in the catalog. It pays because you have become an expert in the art of *learning* to learn. This is indeed your major and also the true thrust of education. What matters is not just *what* you learn but *how* you learn.

Learning to Learn

This emphasis on *how* rather than *what* gives college a new slant. Instead of worrying entirely about what subjects to take, you also consider which courses will help you most with the skills associated with learning, and give you most practice in the art. A college curriculum offers an extraordinary menu of new learning. The more practice you get developing the skills that go with new learning, the easier it will be for you in the future to adapt to new kinds of work.

Over the years I have tried to explain this point to non-college employees who are rising slowly through the ranks and aspire to supervisory positions. They cannot see why the company hires and promotes a young college degree-holder to such a job in preference to themselves who have had years of experience in their lines. The reason is that the old-timer has done his or her particular learning and growing in one discipline only. The process is slow because it is delayed by having to maintain daily bread and butter tasks. One cannot be learning something new on a job every day. The college grad has had several years of continual practice in the skill of learning the *new*. What else is the purpose of reading more books or performing more lab experiments? The student becomes a pro. Having mastered the art, he or she can apply it elsewhere. As the National Center for Research in Vocational Education says, "Learning to learn is itself a skill that transfers."[1]

The Learning Transkills

Thus, *learning* is the key hidden skill that college teaches. It is transferable from discipline to discipline and from one situation to the next. The Transkills Finder (page 13) lists it under the general heading of "Transkills Using the Mind." More particularly, it is associated with the transkills of *gaining knowledge* —

Investigating   *Analyzing*
Researching   *Evaluating*
Memorizing   *Conceptualizing*
Recalling

Some other closely related transkills are —

Gathering data, information, ideas
Compiling data and information
Being logical/reasoning
Synthesizing
Using imagination

All of these can be used in any kind of college-level course. Billy while at high school (p. 92) had already spotted his skill in *analyzing* as a result of his baboon research. Analysis is identifying the parts. Billy examined the slides of the cultures for their different "parts." He said he was thinking that way now and "could stick to it," that is, in another setting.

Conceptualizing is a skill you use to write a paper. You draw from the ideas of several authors; you synthesize their points of view and create an arrangement of your own. It has universal, lifelong application. Astute employers consider it a vital skill for responsible positions.

One of the partners of Coopers & Lybrand, a certified public accounting firm, described this process when asked what you do when you make an audit. He said you go in and look at a system that isn't working, absorb a lot of inputs from different sources, whirl them around, array them in a different framework, and put them together to make the system work. That's *conceptualizing*.

College offers more than opportunities to learn all these mental transkills. The glut of extra-curricular activities allows you to learn and practise skills that involve *relationships with others*. (See last column of the Transkills Finder). You may not realize when you go to the bursar's office to argue about an error in the dormitory bill, or raise an issue with the prof about your grades that you may be showing adeptness in the transkill of *negotiating*. The thing to watch for is whether or not you really enjoy these little episodes. If you go out for the band, chorus, or debating society you ask yourself whether or not you are getting a kick out of being on stage. It could mean you like *performing for others* in the broadest sense. If you plunge into a program of visiting old people, you can immediately begin measuring the degree of enjoyment you're getting from this *helping* role; you think about how well you're carrying it out, too.

However, it's easy to be thrown off the scent. Your friends will still appraise you in terms of your specialty. If you excel in catching forward passes, they will talk about you as a hot forward pass receiver, not as the kind of person who is skillful at being in the right place at the right time.

Acquiring the more sophisticated mental and interpersonal skills, like *conceptualizing, problem solving, negotiating* and *planning* has infelicitous aspects. Educators give no credit to you for learning them or to themselves for teaching them.

Worse, your first job is not likely to demand these skills. As we shall see in the next chapter, employers expect neophytes to learn the company ropes and pull their own weight quickly. Your duties are prescribed;⁰ you are more apt to be using the transkills listed under *attention to detail*. Bosses don't want you to be using your imagination, making suggestions, or thinking big too soon. Later, as your work becomes less prescribed and more complex, they will demand and expect more sophisticated skills.[3] Says the vice-chancellor of the University of Maryland, "The main purpose of the liberal arts education is to prepare a person for his last job rather than his first."⁴ A client reported this experience to me.

> Through my father I got an interview with a top executive. He was very friendly and encouraging. His message: we can use young men like you with a generalist background. He called a department head and asked her to see me. We arranged an interview. She listened attentively to my story. Her message: we must see how you might fit into this organization. She called the personnel manager. At this interview, days later, I was greeted cordially, introduced to an employment interviewer. He reviewed my application form, and described the jobs they were likely to have open — purchasing assistant, sales assistant, salesman, employment recruiter. They didn't sound like "generalist" jobs to me. They each required some particular knowledge I didn't have. They sounded awfully restricted, too.

This experience is normal. The top dog is a model generalist dealing with complex mental processes and people skills. The watch dog at the door is not trying to fill the president's job, only entry-level openings with narrowly prescribed duties.

Immediate Uses

Thus the various mental transkills you develop in college may not pay off the minute you punch in on your first job, but they can, first, wake you up, and second, set you on a course of thinking about your future. Take the process of waking up, or what the trade calls acquiring "awareness."

> A group of liberal arts seniors at Northeastern University were going through the *Searchway*. One of them said she liked some of her studies and had done well in them. Someone suggested analyzing this experience for transkills. Minutes later the group was astounded to discover that as a student she had not only used all the learning skills (p. 96) in these courses, but also: *planning, solving problems, following instructions, setting goals, following through, meeting deadlines, working under pressure, being independent, competing,* and *organizing oneself.* Their instant rejoinders were, "If I had learned about this earlier it would have helped me decide my major," and "If I'd analyzed myself this way in high school, I might have had some idea of what college to go to."

One student went on immediately to act on her revelations.

She had enjoyed various writing courses plus the interchanges in class and campus activity. She'd been able to persuade others of her ideas. She linked up these transkills to the field of public relations. Then, consciously, she used her *influencing* abilities to get an appointment with a visiting campus recruiter who was looking for engineers. Yet she made her p.r. pitch so compelling he referred her to his director of public relations.

Acting on your new awareness ordinarily involves more sustained effort than this flash. The process has to spread through the other STEPS described in the *Searchway* —

Identifying transkills in jobs (STEP 10).
Compiling a list of careers to explore (STEP 11).
Exploring the best of these in information
gathering interviews (STEP 12).

You cannot execute these haphazardly in spare moments. They take time, effort, and commitment. Furthermore, as in any course of study, you need resources.

Fortunately, a number of colleges in the U.S. are now teaching some of the process described in the *Searchway*. The school of career counseling from which the *Searchway* derives and which I call the Haldane-Bolles-Crystal school — authors of the seminal works — has made an impact on college career counseling (see Resources).

At Columbia University since 1970 students have been joining the "DIG" seminar which helps them search for their successful accomplishments and the transferable skills used. Ultimately they develop resumes for career fields that exploit their talents.[5] DIG is based on Bernard Haldane's original concept, dating from 1945, that people who are starting or changing careers must look for and be guided by talents they enjoy and use successfully. The data from an outside survey of 200 DIG graduates strongly indicates "that those who have elected to use the DIG program have subsequently experienced employment which has allowed them to use their skill attributes more fully than before, and has provided increased intrinsic and extrinsic rewards at the same salary level as their peers."[6] Enjoying your work does not necessarily mean working for less.

At Dickinson College in Pennsylvania the career counseling staff feels that students should quickly zero in on "values." For instance, you might take a transkill, like *being physically active*, and see in it for yourself the value of maintaining good health; or the value derived from

ability to meet people might be friendliness. The immediate lesson is that these values based on skills are transferable through a wide range of past and present activities
and will be in the future. At this point the student may see
that these values can also be translated across the board
into occupations that appear quite diverse. The staff tries
to bring this message to everyone who walks in the door.
Those who are intrigued with this revelation can sign up
for the total career development process.[7]

Benefits from early career counseling can be measured,
too. Everett College in the state of Washington discovered
that Freshmen who enrolled immediately in the career
planning seminar had a grade point average at the end of
the year of 2.59 differing significantly from the 2.09
average for a group of students who did not.[8]

College counseling offices report that a majority of
students do not put in an appearance in four years; some
don't even know the office's location. The staff at University of Massachusetts' Boston campus has an ally in the
admissions office; prospects are informed of the career
office, shown the location, and introduced. A pamphlet
urges high school guidance counselors to evaluate a college's counseling services before making referrals and
recommendations. At Wellesley College one of the first
officials that first-year foreign students meet is the director of career counseling and placement.

In Michigan, Alma College's aim is to make you aware
of how to use your education, in this case, the liberal arts.[9]
You are expected, but not required, during the four years
to sign up for workshops in skills identification, career
exploration, information-gathering and decision making.
Curriculum stresses learning not only the basic competencies needed for entry-level work, but also the transferable skills needed for lifework. You gain competency in
writing, for instance, through the practising of resume or
project report writing. You learn more about oral com-
munications in workshops on interviewing. The skill that
is being learned is emphasized, not just the end-product.
At the same time you learn the competencies needed for
more responsible positions, *tolerating others' viewpoints,
managing time, analyzing, evaluating* and *conceptualizing.*
Faculty advisors at Alma are trained to discuss this
process with you. They raise the question, "What do you
want to do with yourself, and what skills and knowledge
will you need to do it?" rather than just, "What courses do

you want to take?" There are at least half a dozen other colleges in the U.S. that have integrated the teaching of competencies into the overall curriculum.[10]

The counseling department at Butte Community College in Oroville, California has publicly published a workbook incorporating skills analysis. The process has been used for eight years with students of ages 17 to 68.[11]

Of course you may not find just the college that offers these resources, or you may not like the counselors on site. You may not feel moved, i.e., you're unmotivated. You may ask, "Do I have to do it right now?" Alas, many people do not. But if they at least know there is such a process and vow to use it later, that's a starter.

Self-Instruction Possible?

Can I learn it by myself? The basic premise of the *Searchway* is that you need the support of a friend or group to help you learn and keep you going. Possibly you could teach yourself if you are resolute about making the shift from low to high gear and don't mind starting and stalling. But don't risk learning the key STEPS by yourself (STEPS 1, 2, 3, 4, identification of transkills). Here is where a little constructive dependency works. Completing these steps with others will set you on your way. And this familiarity with your skills pays off in the end when you face the employer.

Once you learn the knack of transkills identification you can develop it on your own like any good habit — dental hygeine, eating fruit and green vegetables, driving carefully, looking before you leap. Once awareness occurs, then you begin asking yourself key questions about your particular actions and behaviors.

You win a debate and ask yourself to what extent it was because you presented the demographic statistics more *persuasively than before.*

You return from a party feeling good about it. Was this just the drinks, or had it anything to do with your being able *to meet and talk with people* more easily?

You discuss in class the surge of popularity for President John F. Kennedy after he announced the Bay of Pigs disaster and for President Jimmy Carter when he announced the aborted rescue of the American hostages in Iran. You suddenly realize that a disaster in foreign affairs, when handled openly, can brighten a presidential image. Is your discovery just happenstance, or are your powers of *seeing parallels* improving? Then, my God! Does that mean that a leader, risking disaster, can count on gaining some popularity from it if he handles it honestly with the public? (A sharpening of your ability to *reason inductively*.)

On your part-time stock clerk job at the supermarket you notice that three fellow-employees occasionally come to you with their troubles and you *listen* gladly. What does this tell you about your skills with people? Could you use it in the future?

Each time your thinking takes this track you add a dimension to your own self-development and self-concept. It takes time and practice. But what might seem like serving time at college can turn into a business of learning to learn and thus learning to grow.

College as a Career

Whether you use the resources available or instruct yourself, there is a trick that will help you realize the benefits of the campus experience: simply view it as a unique career in itself.

Your job title is "student." Your environment is a 100% learning to learn environment. Whichever way you turn you cannot miss. In class you are exercising your *listening* and *oral communication* skills. In the library you are getting practice in *researching, evaluating, memorizing,* and *record keeping*. In the lab you are immersed in *calculating, following directions,* and *inspecting*. In writing papers you specialize in *synthesizing* and *conceptualizing*.

When you consciously make observations like those of the student debater, party-goer, and stock clerk, you are learning to watch your own behavior and hence your development.

All this practice helps you make a better-informed decision when you want to try something different. The risks are relatively low. You can shift your extra-curricular activities quickly. You can change your major; about half of all college students do. Knowing what you like and are good at enables you to cope with the decision to quit, take a leave, or transfer. At least 25% of students entering college are transfers.

If you view college as a career in itself, you can also view your first year on a regular job a little differently. You can think of it as an extension of your college career — a practicum in which you are getting some on-the-job experience in applying those college-developed transkills. You will be able to discern which skills you are using well and enjoying and which you are not.

In conclusion, the college career is expensive and time-consuming, but unique. Although the job of "student" is not listed as an occupation, it can indeed be a productive one.

FOOTNOTES

1. Nina Selz and William L. Ashley, *Teaching for Transfer: A Perspective* (Columbus: National Center for Research in Vocational Education, Ohio State University, 1978), p. 12.

2. Sidney A. Fine and Wretha W. Wiley, *An Introduction to Functional Job Analysis* (Washington, D.C.: W.E. Upjohn Institute for Employment Research, 1971), p. 20.

3. George O. Klemp Jr., "Career Development and Job Competency," presented at annual meeting of American Council on Education, October, 1977. McBer & Co., 137 Newbury St., Boston, Mass.

   Kenneth B. Hoyt, "Career Education and Liberal Arts Education," speech at Emmanuel College, Boston, October 22, 1977.

4. "Panelists Discuss Liberal Education," American Personnel and Guidance Association *Guidepost*, Feb. 17, 1977, p.2.

5. Richard M. Gummere, Jr., *How to Survive Education* (New York: Harcourt Brace Jovanovich, 1971), Chapter 18, pp. 149-158.

   Richard M. Gummere, Jr., "DIG/Columbia University's Program to Help Students Find Answers," *Journal of College Placement*, April-May 1972.

6. Allen A. Wiant, *Self-Assessment for Career Change. Does it Really Work?* (Columbus: National Center for Research in Vocational Education, Ohio State University, 1979), p. 33.

7. Howard E. Figler, "How to Counsel Students When They Offer You Only an Hour of Their Time," *Journal of College Placement*, Fall, 1974, pp. 33-40.

   Howard E. Figler, *PATH: A Career Workbook for Liberal Arts Students* (Cranston, R.I.: Carroll, 1975), pp. 54-56.

8. Glenn A. Adams, "Preventive Counseling," *Journal of College Placement*, Spring 1974, pp. 27-33.

9. Daniel W. Behring, *Career Preparation and the Liberal Arts* (Alma, Mich.: Alma College, 1979).

10. Alverno College, Milwaukee, Wis.; Kirkhoff College of Grand Valley State College, Allendale, Mich.: Mars Hill College, Mars Hill, N.C.; Metropolitan State Junior College, St. Paul, Wis.; University Studies, University of Nebraska, Lincoln, Neb.; Our Lady of the Lake College, San Antonio, Tex.

11. Edmond Billingsley, *Career Planning and Job Hunting for Today's Student: The Nonjob Interview Approach* (Santa Monica: Goodyear, 1978).

RESOURCES

Seminal Works

Bolles, Richard N. *What Color is Your Parachute?* Berkeley: Ten Speed, 1980. Original Edition 1972.

Crystal, John C. and Richard N. Bolles, *Where Do I Go from Here with my Life?* New York, Seabury, 1974.

Haldane, Bernard, *How to Make a Habit of Success.* Washington, D.C.: Acropolis, 1975. Original Edition 1960.

11

Getting the First Job

You, as a newcomer to the employment scene, are disadvantaged. Our hiring "system" actually operates against you. You need a special technique to overcome your handicap and get your foot in the door. This chapter describes your disadvantage and what you can do in the early stages of your job search to overcome it.

The Non-System

When you set out to seek your first regular job you may have the notion that some system exists to link you up with the employer. There seems to be evidence all around. Newspapers run classified ads; employment agencies broadcast their services; employers welcome you with signs labelled "Employment" or "Personnel." Inside, there are lobbies, tables and chairs, application blanks, receptionists and interviewers awaiting you.

You soon find this machinery isn't working for you. Your friends report it failed them, too. "I saw an ad and sent in my resume; no one answered . . ." "The employment interviewer never called back . . ." "The Personnel Office said they had no openings . . ." "The receptionist said the job had just been filled." You wonder: if the methods that newspapers, agencies, and employers themselves promote do not work, what system are you supposed to use?

The incredible truth is that in spite of our advanced technology, productivity, and sophisticated concerns for people we have never been able to develop a systematic way to match people to jobs. There is no such mechanism that works simultaneously on behalf of both parties. The "labor market" you read so much about simply does not exist. There is no public place where employers can market their needs and wares, or where you can market yours.[1] This means each of you — applicant and employer — is out shopping on his own, searching valiantly for the other.

Why is this? It's worthwhile to understand what actually does go on before you set out on your pilgrimage. Let's examine, first, the employer's point of view and actions in the early stages of the hiring process, then yours, and finally mesh the two.

Employers' Approach

The term "employers" needs defining. I use it throughout to refer to all organizations that employ people, including employers in the profit and non-profit sectors, education, and government.

Employers regard people as one — and only one — of several resources they must juggle to provide a product or a service. The other resources are also crucial to them — money, information, and physical things like materials, equipment, and facilities. For instance, if money gives out you may not get promoted, but demoted or laid off instead; as for a job, you'd never even get near it. If the employer is gobbled up by another, or has to move facilities, you may be out, too. Note the contrast to school. Educators view you as the end-product; employers do not. Their end is a product or a service.

All employers face an unpredictable element — the people they serve or service. Customs, fashions, events, population shifts, and wars change people's needs and demands. Employers adjust, and the adjusting may hurt you as an employee. You are dispensable; you go. And, of course, in the end you go anyway; you retire.

If employers view people in this way as dispensable, then they are not overly concerned whether or not you in particular get a job. They simply want to fill vacancies with "people" resources. Here's how it works:

The boss, Mary, has an opening. She is busy with her own operation; looking for a new recruit is an unwelcome and time-consuming interruption. She wants the "right" person fast. She delegates the task to someone else, say John, the employment man.

John aims to find some likely applicants with the least time, effort, and money. He wants to interview as few as possible yet produce a pool of "qualified" applicants from which Mary can select one. John has a handy formula to produce applicants with the right job qualifications. It will solve the problem quickly. It is:

$$JQ = ED + EX$$

where **JQ** = Job qualifications
where **ED** = Education
where **EX** = Experience

In order to adapt it to his situation he merely has to quantify it. Mary has told him to get someone with experience so that she will not have to spend her time, effort, and money training the new recruit. She wants instant productivity. They figure that means 2 years experience. And the right quantity of education is 4 years of college. For this job, then, the job qualification formula reads:

$$JQ = 4ED + 2EX$$

Like any formula it yields an exact answer which for efficency sake is what John wants. It lets him accept for interviewing the applicants who qualify with 4ED + 2EX. It lets him screen out those who do not. Moreover, he can reject these unqualified applicants with a rationale. People understand the terminology "education" and "experience." They accept the terms being quantified like the rules of a ballgame: 3 strikes, you're out! 4 downs without a 10-yard gain, you lose the ball.

The United States Civil Service Commission sets an example for this treatment. Here is an excerpt from a pamphlet, *Working for the USA*: "Before you apply, read the announcement carefully. If the announcement says that only persons who have 1 year of experience along certain lines will qualify and you don't have that experience, don't apply."

Easy as pie. 10 months of experience only — you're out!

This method of screening by **ED** and **EX** is virtually universal. Employers see it as an efficient way to cut down the pool of applicants in which to fish. For you it appears to be an insurmountable barrier; even though you might have the education, you cannot possibly have the experience. How do you get around that? Before we answer let's turn to your angle.

Your Approach

As you commence your search you realize that the "system" is not working for you. Indeed, only 5 out of 100 people who walk into a private employment agency get placed; in two large cities only 20-25% of employers hire anyone through classified ads.[2] As you talk to others who've gone through this ordeal you find they don't rely on these publicized methods. They initiate their own contacts through friends or teachers or with the employer directly.

My daughter and friends conducted a little survey among 53 acquaintances and asked how they found their jobs. 57% said they found out through word of mouth or their own contacting of employers, not through formal, publicized means like ads and agencies. The Department of Labor asked 10 million people the same question. 63% had found jobs on their own without using ads or agencies.[3]

Getting a job through personal rather than impersonal contacts is often referred to cynically: "It's whom you know." No need to be cynical. If you already know someone, and he or she helps in giving you a lead, of course, that's an inside boost. Use it! But these people who get jobs through personal contact also include those who set out to *find* and *know* that right person. In fact 35% of those 10,000,000 simply walked in off the street, asked for, and found that person to know; and that person listened to them. They were not just "lucky."

Personal contacting is an example of one of many techniques you need to use in job hunting if you are going to synchronize your search with the employers'. As noted in Chapter 7, this book does not describe all these techniques; the books that do are listed at the end of that chapter. Your job hunt requires such a text.

But there is one piece of information you already have that can guide you in every phase of job-hunting; it can give you the confidence to succeed. This is the information you gathered about your transkills in STEPS 1, 2, 3, and 4 of the *Searchway* (see summary on page 55). It is the backbone of the entire process and carries right through the job hunt. Richard Bolles advocates knowledge of one's transferable skills as an absolute essential. He wrote me:

> I have for years refused to interview anyone on the basis of their resume. Rather, I have required of each applicant that they write a one-page paper on the subject of "What are the skills you most enjoy using which you hope this job will utilize?" It is amazing, to me, how even the supposedly unsophisticated (in the concept of skills) are able to write a very intelligent page when they know the issue of *enjoy* is at stake.

It is this ingredient — your enjoyed skills — that is going to forge the link between your needs and the employers'. If you do not have the ED and EX the employer says are required, you are going to have to rely on your transkills.

By now you may be agreeing with this new method of exploiting your transkills to get around the ED + EX requirement, but that does not mean that everyone else does.

The National Center for Research in Vocational Education points out a weakness of skills identification: employers do not describe their jobs in the same terms.[4]

A job counselor in a CETA placement office railed at me after taking my skills identification seminar, "What use is it for the applicant to know his transkills, if the guy who's interviewing has never heard of them?"

A personnel manager I know gags when he sees a resume which starts off by stressing the applicant's transferable skills rather than a neat, chronological experience record. "Everyone's using this gimmick now," he says. Of course he doesn't like these skills-oriented resumes because he needs and wants to hire only people who already have the right experience. Why bother with those who don't?

A few employers, however, have made sporadic attempts to use transferable skills in order to encourage and recruit the inexperienced. These attempts do not appear to have been systematically institutionalized.

In World War II Polaroid advertised for polarized lens polishers. The job required "unusual skills in *hand operations* demonstrated by . . . hobbies like violin playing, model building, and needlework."

In the early days of computer programming IBM's developers knew the art would demand powers of *logical reasoning*. The legend is they advertised, "chess players wanted." The master spy, Intrepid, also recruited chess players to crack the Nazis' "Enigma" coding machine.

Recently Microwave advertised that the requirements for entry-level assembly were quite basic — "good eye sight, *attention to detail*, and *manual dexterity*. Are you talented at sewing, knitting, painting, piano playing?" And a newpaper clipping service advertised for people who *worked well with their hands* and might have had experience with knitting, sewing or ceramics.

Recruiters for Jordan Marsh's department store in Boston tell students that a salesperson should *work well under pressure*. Proof, they suggest, could be playing on a basketball team, working for a political candidate, debating, and juggling a lot of assignments at one time.

Another department store, Abraham & Straus in Brooklyn, asks prospects to rate themselves on *analytical skills* they could use in solving problems.

Atlantic Richfield once used a recruiting brochure that asked you to name some skills you learned in college or from extra-curricular activities, like *written communication* or *grasping new concepts*.

Friendly's employment manager told me they like to hire basketball players for behind the counter. *Fast footwork* and *good balance* enable them to scoop icecream, spin around, and get it to the customer fast without bumping others. (In Studs Terkel's *Working*, the waitress describes how she has to move deftly between tables and chairs: "I feel like a ballerina.")[5]

Employers in Cincinnati collaborated with the CETA placement services in using a unique checklist of life experiences common to people working on semi- and unskilled jobs. This checklist asked the applicants to what degree he or she (1) had liked and (2) had actually performed 120 everyday tasks, both of a work and non-work variety. A computer converted the applicant's preferred and performed tasks into the transkills used. The same process was applied to the most frequently vacated semi- and unskilled jobs in the city. The applicants with the appropriate transkills were then matched to the jobs that used these skills.[6]

These examples of employers using transkills as a recruiting technique are exceptions. Generally, you will have to take that initiative yourself.

Here are some "success stories" which have to be oversimplified in the telling. They are not intended to give the impression that the people jumped into ideal occupations the minute they became aware of their transkills. Of course, their special preferences, wishes, and musts (i.e., STEPS 5 to 9, pp. 27-39) came into play, too. But these vignettes do illustrate how the individuals understood their transkills and were able to translate them effectively to someone else.

A high schooler trained in typing was aware she enjoyed doing and operating things with her hands, like cake decorating and typing. But actually to work as a typist did not seem satisfying. She heard about a machine apprentice program at a steel fabricating plant. She took the recruiting tour and watched a machinist on a lathe. She told them she liked working with her hands, operating a machine as she had the typewriter, and especially making something. She got the job as machinist apprentice.

A liberal arts senior at Columbia University stated on her resume that her job objective was to be a research writer "dealing with theoretical ideas and concepts." A paper she wrote on Descartes had demonstrated her abilities to analyze, synthesize, and write concisely and cogently. She wound up with a job in market research, which is a far cry from philosophy but deals with lots of analysis, synthesis, writing, and theoretical ideas about why people buy!

Jonas, another senior, reported these experiences in a workshop — telling stories, getting people together from different backgrounds, gaining the confidence of Eskimo children. But then he disappeared. A year later he showed up to thank the staff. Sorry he hadn't finished the program but he'd got what he needed. He'd decided on ministry school.[7] The skills he had used in each experience — *holding people's attention, giving talks* (called "preaching" in the profession), *getting consensus, inspiring confidence* — had contributed to that decision.

Two young women, one a high school and one a college grad, used their successful experiences as baby sitters to emphasize their ability to *deal with unexpected people situations* (involving both children and adults), to help *solve problems for others*, and, in general, to *take care of people's needs*. One landed a job as a receptionist in a small town hospital; the other as an assistant in a high school counseling program two years after she had taken the *Searchway* seminar and had tried various jobs. She wrote, "It is so amazing — out of that brainstorming session someone had suggested 'counseling' for me!"

To sum it up, the key to getting your first job, when you have no specific education or experience for it, is to pin down your transkills. This firm knowledge that you do indeed possess such talents and have proved them will carry you through the many succeeding steps of your job search. When you reach the point when you find that right person to "know" and talk to, preferably the one who understands the job first-hand, look to your transkills to sell you. That person will see the link between them and the job.

FOOTNOTES

1. Richard Lathrop, *Who's Hiring Who* (Berkeley: Ten Speed, 1977), pp. 3 and 16.

2. Richard N. Bolles, *The Three Boxes of Life* (Berkeley: Ten Speed, 1978), p. 270.

3. U.S. Department of Labor, *Jobseeking Methods Used by American Workers* (Washington, D.C.: Bureau of Labor Statistics, 1975), p. 7.

4. Allen A. Wiant & Ronald Hutchinson, *Self Assessment for Career Change: Does It Really Work?* (Columbus: National Center for Research in Vocational Education, Ohio State University, 1979), p. 2.

5. Studs Terkel, *Working* (New York, Random House, 1974), p. 297.

6. Henry G. Pearson, "A 'Total Skills' Approach to Placement," *Industry*, Associated Industries of Massachusetts, June 1979, p. 30.

7. Richard M. Gummere, Jr., "DIG/Columbia University's Program to Help Students Find Answers." *Journal of College Placement*, April-May 1972.

12

During the Work Years

We have all been dissatisfied at some time with our jobs. Complaining about them comes easy; we can usually pick on something or someone other than ourselves.

For instance, you are bound to become disenchanted with your boss, and why not? You may weary of taking abrupt orders; or being asked to do something you don't do, or don't want to do, or don't do too well. But then, that's the boss's job. Bosses wouldn't be needed if everything went OK.

Or perhaps your communication is non-existent.

> A recently hired engineer called up Carl in the personnel office and abruptly announced he was going to quit. "It's my boss," he said. Then that boss called Carl and said he just could not understand it. "What did you say to him?" Carl asked. "Nothing, nothing at all. That's just the point. I've hardly had time to speak to him since I hired him."

Or possibly your communication is all one-way and negative:

> "Dirty looks from my boss are common. Never in nine months has anyone come right out and said, 'Could you do it this way? I much prefer it.' That's too easy. The method is not to tell you; just to talk about what a lousy job you are doing."[1]

Another source of dissatisfaction is pay. In all my years in personnel and compensation work I have never seen any pay system that really does what it is supposed to do — compensate you "fairly." This includes not only the 13 employers with whom I have been connected, but also several hundred that I have dealt with or surveyed.

> In the U.S. Air Force I was a corporal working with statistics. I noticed one day the commanding general's chauffeur had been promoted to sergeant — sporting three stripes to my two. I went to the executive officer, saluted, pointed out the discrepancy, saluted and retired. Next month I had my own three stripes.

All organizations are riddled with such inequities. Most of them are built into the ranking system and cannot be budged with a mere salute.

You may also be disgruntled with the way your boss evaluates how *well* you are performing. To you it's clear that on sheer merit you are worth more. But the boss also has to weigh your worth against others' and take into account the budget for merit raises. There is never enough money in it to go around; you may be the one to miss out.

Another irksome factor is overload. Some employers overload you on purpose; that way they make a profit from working you more than you're paid for; others overload you because of tight budgeting or inefficiency. Even though you love your work, perpetual overload can get you down.

A more subtle cause for a beginner's dissatisfaction is that the newness of the job may wear off. When you first come on board you may enjoy meeting new people, settling into a new environment, picking up new rules and customs, and mastering new tasks. It's like the pleasure you get from traveling; each day brings new experiences. This break-in period is unadulterated *learning*. But the boss can't provide it *ad infinitum*. The day comes when you have mastered your tasks and you have a full-time job performing them. The learning bloom fades. Just when this transition results in boredom only you can judge — weeks, months, years, or in **stages?**

Then it could be that you are one of those people who really do not want to be bossed at all. It is indeed one of the hazards of working for someone else.

> A friend of mine who had been manager successively of a textile mill, engineering group, and personnel department told me it took him all these experiences over a period of years to admit that he really did not want to work for anyone. Now he's happily on his own.
>
> Another friend always developed chest pains as he transferred through various junior management positions. Finally he correlated the chest pains with bosses who breathed down his neck. Now he's found a position where he can feel neither the breath nor the pain.

Finally, there are your co-workers. It's too much to expect to work continuously only with people whom you like. There are always nuisances around to bother you. They can help spoil a job for you, too. All of these are complaints where it is easy to lay the blame elsewhere.

Another kind of complaint, which you might also like to pin on others, has to do with your own advancement. But it is so wrapped up with your future and what you want to do with it that you cannot attribute all the fault to someone else. You are going to have to look deeper than a bad boss or an inequitable pay system. That means you must re-appraise yourself.

Re-Appraising Yourself

This re-appraisal, of course, starts by reviewing your greatest strengths — your transkills — to determine whether or not you are using them on your job. Following the procedures of the *Searchway,* STEPS 1-4 (pp. 2-26), you bring up to date your list of enjoyed experiences and skills on and off the job. Be sure to log any pleasant tasks, no matter how slight, on your present job. They count as experiences and may produce some significant transkills you were not totally aware of.

Sometimes such reviews convince people that they are not as unhappy as they imagine.

Beth, a potential defector from hotel and restaurant management, realizes she nevertheless loves the hurly-burly of people every minute of the day. She revels in the new contacts and demands placed on her. It's a real "people intensive" job. She decides she likes this way of being busy. Her restlessness subsides.

A medical x-ray technician was giving me an intravenous pylogram. Between pictures I asked her how she liked her job. It was the kind of reply Studs Terkel reports in *Working.*[2] "So, so. It's like most any job. Some days I like it; some days I don't. I've learned about all I can now." After another shot I asked what other skills she used besides her know-how of x-ray procedures. She ducked behind the screen again, and then reappeared to report, "Well, the patients. You know . . ." and she told how she explained to them what was happening, made them comfortable, and lessened their anxiety. I could attest to it. Later when I walked out in my johnny I said, "That's quite an art, handling patients, isn't it?" She reflected, then said, "I guess I feel better about my job today." But this time she knew why.

A harassed math teacher was thinking of quitting when he uncovered the rewarding element in teaching which compensated for all the hassle: the glow he felt when he succeeded in getting through to the student. He decided to stay put.

All three had discovered the satisfaction they got and the proficiency they acquired from the people component of their work.

But perhaps your self-review indicates that your present situation does not allow you the upward mobility you want. Then you are faced with one of the most difficult feats in the art of human relationships — a productive interview with your boss. In other words, if you want to do something about getting ahead — whether by promotion, transfer, or modification of your duties — you must sooner or later present your case to the principal person who can help you.

Tackling the Boss

See your boss? Take the initiative? All management, personnel and labor relations people, and their publications urge this primary strategy. I do, too. Admittedly, it's easy for the "experts" to espouse this initiative as a matter of policy. But for an employee to venture such a step for the first time is quite another matter.

A woman working in a university said, "I had something important I wanted to tell my boss about my work. But she always looks so busy I hate to interrupt."

"When I go to my supervisor's office," says a mechanical inspector, "he waves me into a chair. Then the phone rings. He keeps answering it instead of talking to me."

A teacher says, "If I tell my boss in advance I want to see her, she says, 'OK, I'll get back to you.' But she doesn't."

There isn't an employee who hasn't had qualms about seeing the boss. And don't think the reticence is limited to people at the bottom. The education director of the National Association of Bank Women says one reason why there are so few women in top bank jobs is that many of those who are qualified with good banking experience hesitate to ask their employers for the training they need to advance to senior management positions.[3]

Another deterrent may be making the assumption that the boss will be negative about your thoughts.

"I want to ask my boss if I could attend certain

meetings," says a supervisor. "I'm afraid he won't like it though. Then I'm in the dog house."

That's an unfair premise if it's your first try. At least give the boss a chance to hear you.

At all levels of organization the boss attends to the crises of the moment first. Heart-to-heart talks with subordinates are deferrable. You're put off. This consistently low-priority treatment of your needs gets through to you; you give up the effort to pull off the interview.

> Civil War general, "Old Rosey" Rosencrans, had a password when he saw a soldier with worn-out shoes: "Go to your Captain and demand what you need. Go to him every day till you get it. Bore him for it in his quarters, at meal time, in his bed. Don't let him rest."[4]

You will need some of this persistence to raise the issue of your skills. Remember your under-used skills are your worn-out shoes. Demand a new pair!

Negotiating Internal Change

In approaching your boss remember you have a right to do so. Make a date when the calendar is free. You do not need to bill this talk as a complaint — simply a discussion about your future. (You could have done it before you were hired. So why not now?) Agreeing on the date and topic gives both of you a chance to think about the matter in advance.

The way to start the interview, then, is not with a negative comment about the job, or even a challenging question like "Where can I go in this organization?" Instead, you begin by talking positively on a subject you know more about than anyone else — your assets, especially your transkills. Your knowledge of how much or little you use them is obviously first-hand. You can speak convincingly because they are the skills you excel in and enjoy.

You can also be sure that what you have to say is news. Bosses are not familiar with what tasks and skills you enjoy. They never ask; nor is it customary for you to report them.

> Susan was a Polaroid secretary who felt she was at a dead-end. But she liked the job and did not really want to quit. She took the seminar in skills identification and confirmed to herself that she was competent with figures and enjoyed working with them. She made a date with her boss. After pointing out the transkills she used effectively as a secretary, she told him she'd found she liked figure work. He was surprised (women are not supposed

to like arithmetic). She asked if there were any tasks she could do involving figures. He nodded and handed over the section's budget book and said he'd show her how to pull together the quarterly revisions to the budget. Her career problem, at least for the time being, was solved. She was now utilizing a neglected talent; the boss was giving her recognition for it.

Susan had spoken with conviction; she imparted new information about herself. More important, she took the initiative. Most bosses, as I noted earlier, are swamped with just getting the job done every day. They are not sitting around thinking about how everyone's talents could be better used. Even if they had the time, they could not figure it out because they do not know what skills identification is. So you have to do it yourself.

Once you have disclosed your evaluation of your transkills, you have actually made the boss's response easier. Now he or she does not have to come up with a neat evaluation of his or her own — always a difficult task. Instead the boss can ask questions and make comments about your evaluation — always easier. Of course, these ideas may not jibe with yours, but then, you might learn something from the interchange, too.

The strategy, then, is to find out, just as Susan did, how you can use your transkills better right where you are. A small shift in tasks and skills may be enough to satisfy you. You may already have your own ideas; or you may get help from the boss or a colleague.

A high school counselor who spent all day talking one-to-one with students felt his job was tying him to his desk too much. He had learned enough about skills identification to realize that he shone whenever he was greeting people and handling their inquiries and complaints. (His dream job was to run a motel.) He suggested to the director that he serve one day a week as receptionist and inquiry-handler for all kids who came in the door. He explained to his boss why he was good at this and got the OK. This one-day-a-week shift benefited everyone. Students who merely had quick questions got quick answers; other counselors were saved these interruptions; he enjoyed himself.

A computer programmer liked developing new programs for clients but chafed at routine inquiries he had to handle regularly for other members of the firm. The duty got so irksome he explored his options. He inquired about his future with the firm and investigated his favorite recreation — canoeing and camping guidework. The latter would harness his physical and outdoor talents, but put out to pasture his abilities in reasoning. He opted for another less radical move, starting his own programming consultancy.

A group of CETA "outreach" interviewers were visiting elderly people each day. One delighted in putting together the names and addresses for the week and locating them on the map. Another disliked this paperwork and wanted to make as many visits as possible. When they happened to discover these preferences, they did some swapping with their boss's OK. One made up the lists for both; the other took on extra calls.

Incidentally, small modifications may be more acceptable to management than proposals for big changes. Traditionally, the changes most workers make over a lifetime are miniscule. When they occur they consist of minor re-assignments, one-step promotions, and fractional increases in pay.[5] Bosses are used to thinking this way about people getting ahead. They can grasp a request to make a minor adjustment, and it is usually within their jurisdiction to handle.

There are others who through re-appraisal and consultation will discover themes in their lives that later lead to solid promotions.

Two bench assemblers in a high technology plant in New Hampshire were stuck as "non-exempt" blue collar workers. They wanted to break through the barrier to become "exempt" white collar workers on salary. One described with great delight how she had taken over balancing the check book from her husband who botched it every month. She brought it in. It was elegantly neat; it always balanced out the first time around. She suddenly heard a clear theme song; it was *handling figures*.

The other discovered that her tune was *being organized and orderly*. It had cropped up in a temporary bank job, her housework, and especially hanging out the family wash. She always hung socks, underwear, and linen in their proper categories. Like her benchmate, she could see how such an asset could be parlayed some day into an exempt job.

A year later the check book balancer wound up in the office of marketing administration juggling all kinds of data. The other was promoted to the office which keeps control over the flow of production, a function that demands a high sense of order. Both, over this period of time, had discussed their skills and desires with their bosses, personnel representatives, and prospective bosses.

A machine operator who liked manufacturing always got a kick out of presenting problems at plant meetings and persuading people to agree on solutions. His boss knew about this knack, so did personnel, and the safety department. Now he is a plant safety officer. He has a full-time job influencing employees and supervisors to work safely.

If You Quit

When you've exhausted the possibilities for advancement, transfer, or modification of duties, then, and only then, are you ready to make the decision to quit. Every book on this subject and every employment counselor urges you to stay put until you have another job. Being out of a job when you are looking for a job places you at a disadvantage. Being employed, whether you think so or not, is seen by potential employers as a measure of success. You'll have some income so you won't have to grab at the first offer; you can plan and pursue a more thorough job search.

At this point you will need to clarify whether you are going to look for the same kind of work; or something quite different; or a little of both.

If you are looking for another job in the same field, you'll be exploiting the experience you already have. You will not have to rely solely on your transferable skills.

If you want to change your line of work, then the exploration of your transkills becomes top priority. This pilgrimage from one career to another follows the same route of self-appraisal and review.

Of course the most dramatic cases of career change occur when the individuals act immediately on the discovery of their talents, talk to their employers, and quite soon find themselves new ones.

A personnel staffer who interviewed applicants for the data processing department went through STEPS 1 to 3 in a group in two hours. At the end of the session she announced, "I'm in the wrong job! I'm really a data person." Not long after she found a job as a computer programmer trainee.

The principal of a high school came to a similar conclusion. Daily he was in contact with his staff, a faculty of 27, many of the 400 students, and frequently their parents

— a people intensive job. He participated in the *Search-way* with the faculty. At the end of the first session he commented to the group, "I don't have a single experience involving people!" By the start of the next school year he had an ideal position developing uniform curricula for a 10-facility school district. The key skill required was *planning* not *people-handling.*

And this musician below had no boss except himself to confer with, but had the sense to consult with friends and a career counselor.

Joe, a percussionist and manager of a three-piece band for 15 years, says, "I've had it. No more music for me." But he relishes selling band time to skeptical restaurant owners. He also relishes his successes with the stock market after a late breakfast each morning. After a stab at selling water beds, he is now an insurance agent. He is using his *promotional* and *numbers* skills to the hilt.

These immediate results, though, are not as significant to me as the fact that these people acquired a new competency. They now know how to ask themselves at any time two questions: "What do I do successfully and enjoyably? What transkills do I use when so doing?" Their answers can serve as a sure-fire guide to new directions they are considering taking.

Testing Values

In your search you will, of course, have other factors to consider. You do not just jump from transkills to the ideal job. You should also review STEPS 5 to 9 (pp. 35-39) — your preferences, goals, priorities — just as the people described above did. In particular, STEP 7 challenges you to ask what your chief satisfactions are and how they relate to the values you hold. I mentioned earlier that identification of values should follow identification of skills. There is a reason.

If we start off by speculating about our values without searching for evidence, we may claim some values that we think we prize but actually may not do much about.

A woman, working on STEP 7, had just checked her life experiences for satisfactions. She said, "I always thought I treasured intellectual activities like philosophizing about life with other people. But I don't see it here. How come?" A minute later she scratched this value for lack of evidence. It was not one of her "must" values.

What she had described was more like an activity and environment she liked and felt comfortable in — an important factor when selecting one's work surroundings and colleagues. It was definitely a high priority STEP 5 "like." As to the moral: check what you say your values are against your experiences for the proof. Be sure to distinguish which are truly operational with you and which are not.

There are always exceptions to rules. Here is a value you might hold and act on and yet not find in your enjoyable experiences — duty. You do certain things because you ought to, not because you especially enjoy them.

> Charles was asked to become a member of his church's vestry committee. He was an enthusiastic church-goer but did not want to serve on any kind of committee. He gave the chairman a reluctant "Yes." When his term of office was over, he breathed one sigh of relief and one of satisfaction. He had performed his duty.

There is certainly no harm in your doing some things you don't like from a sense of duty; you are, in a sense, "enjoying" doing your duty. But don't confuse it with the tasks you performed while doing it.

Actions to Overcome Gaps

Another key exercise to review is STEP 12, Sampling Career Directions. Remember on the form (p. 66) you jotted down the "actions" you could take if you decided to pursue a particular career direction. These actions were aimed at making up whatever you lacked for this particular career.

A common way to compensate for such a lack is further education. Friends, parents, bosses, colleagues, and advisors will urge it on you as a matter of course. More education, in their view, cannot hurt anyone. But bear in mind, they may not know any other advice to give! So, if at this time you are not eager to go back to school, wait a while until you are.

If, or when, you do decide to go, then you need to answer these basic questions first:

1) How much of a "student" am I? Which "student" skills noted on page 96 can I claim?

2) When I took formal courses, what marks did I get? When I got good marks was I also enjoying the course? When I got poor marks, was I really trying my hardest, or was I just not motivated?

3) How many experiences from my STEP 1 require *learning* skills?

Your answers should help you figure out how extensive an education program you should undertake. If your answers lead you to decide you have the makings of a student, then you will feel more confident about this new undertaking; you'll feel surer that you can do well and enjoy it.

If you conclude that you are really not a student, but must compensate for some basic deficiencies anyway — for instance handling words or numbers — then locate a course or a tutor to take care of those handicaps. If going back to school makes you anxious (as it's likely to), warm up with a course you think you'll do well in. There's time for the tougher ones later.

Starting in easily will give you practice in studying; with a little practice you might be encouraged to try harder courses. This approach also helps you decide at what rate you want to continue and how far you want to go. It gives you the chance to switch studies if you find you are not on the right track.

Handling your education this way allows you to acquire the essential knowledge that *you* have decided you need. You can do it before, during, or after the job search. Employers will often hire you when you are merely launching your studies. You are demonstrating to them your motivation.

Learning as you go gives you one advantage over college students, who, without work experience, are plowing the academic fields but getting no chance to employ the skills they learn. Adults at work who have chosen the right courses can often apply at once what they're learning. And sometimes they bring back into the classroom some experiences they can apply to their studies. This instant feedback achieves what some educators say to be the mission of education — *to learn how to make use of one's education.*

Sometimes, in order to achieve your educational objectives, you may be required to take a course you see no use for. You know you will not like it. Here the trick is to grit your teeth and keep your eye on the satisfaction you will get from passing that course. When it's over you simply log this feat as an unpleasant task you were able to bull through. You might want to give it a positive label, *self-discipline.*

This philosophy of getting your satisfactions mainly from end-results can help you in your job-search, too. The job-search is like setting yourself up in a little business. You are on your own; you have to use some skills you are weak in. Very few people possess all the transkills useful in this business of job hunting. Most books overlook this drawback; they just exhort you to go ahead and do it!

Howard Figler in *The Complete Job-Search Handbook*[6] faces this reality. He names 20 skills you need, and few can claim them all. For instance, as the title of my book implies, you need the skills of a detective to dig out lists of contacts and job tips. In the Transkills Finder, page 13, these appear as *investigating* and *researching*. You also need skills in *communicating, listening,* and *asserting* yourself. You'll want *writing* for letters and resumes; and *negotiating* if you have to haggle over pay.

Some of these may lie in your inventory, and others not. If your STEPS 1 to 4 have not revealed *assertiveness,* you may want to read a little about this subject in Figler's *Handbook* (pp. 188-197) or in Bolles's *Parachute* (p. 104). If you feel you need allies, keep your *Searchway* group going and model it on the support group suggested by Figler (pp. 221-229); or find a formal one in your own area (Bolles, 271-272).

If you cannot write easily, look up some model letters and resumes (see Chapter 7, Resources). If you are not high on planning ahead and prefer to jump in, back off anyway, and make a stab at some advance work.

The pain of these few teeth-gritting tasks will be more than offset by your first-hand knowledge that you have a repertory of talents in which you shine. You are on a voyage of discovery to find where they can be used. Put less romantically, you have your clues in hand and are out to solve your own career puzzle.

FOOTNOTES

1. Patricia A. Renwick and Edward E. Lawler, "What You Really Want from your Job," *Psychology Today,* May 1978, p. 58.
2. Studs Terkel, *Working* (New York: Pantheon, 1972).
3. *The Christian Science Monitor,* October 10, 1979.
4. Bruce Catton, *Never Call Retreat* (New York: Doubleday, 1965), p. 37.
5. H.C. White, *Chains of Opportunity* (Cambridge: Harvard University, 1970), pp. 5-6.
6. Howard Figler, *The Complete Job-Search Handbook* (New York: Holt, Rinehard and Winston, 1979), pp. 11-14.

RESOURCES

Adult Learning

Knowles, Malcolm. *The Modern Practice of Adult Education.* New York: Association Press, 1970. Chapters 2 and 3.

Knowles, Malcolm. *Self-Directed Learning.* New York: Association Press, 1975. Part I, "The Learner," pp. 9-28.

Bosses and Organizations

Weiler, Nicholas W. *Reality and Career Planning.* Reading, Mass.: Addison-Wesley, 1977. Ch. 1, "Career Realities," and Ch. 2, "Organization Realities," pp. 9-22.

Solving Job Problems by Skills Analysis

Germann, Richard and Peter Arnold, *Bernard Haldane Associates' Job & Career Building.* New York: Harper & Row, 1980. Ch. 3, pp. 24-38.

13

When Retiring

Retirement brings you a chunk of newly-created freed-up time, your newest asset. What you do with the time deserves to be chosen well.

You choose well by choosing something you know you will enjoy. And you do this by using the same techniques you used in your adult work life to find or change a career.

You also choose well by choosing freely. Your choices before were often influenced by the demands of spouse, family, friends, and bosses. Now you are free to select, first and foremost, something that *you* want to do.

You will find that when you choose freely, you will be a long way towards enjoying your choice. Free personal choice enhances interest; interest enhances enjoyment; and enjoyment enhances the motivation to become more involved and successful.

All very well, but you ask, "what about the limitations placed on me by health and reduced income?" Of course I am talking about making choices that may be restricted. So were the choices you made starting your career or changing it. There are always compromises and trade-offs to be made in important life decisions.

The issue is that within these limits you have at least 40+ hours a week more time at your disposal; and you have the opportunity to decide what to do with it. If you do not take charge now, other influences, especially inertia, will take over and make the decisions for you.

Still, you do not need to balloon this coming freedom into a crisis. Finance, health and housing are indeed problems to cope with. But use of free time should not be perceived as a problem. It is a pleasure to be enjoyed; the choosing of what to do with it should be a pleasure, too.

Many gerontologists and authors on aging refer to this kind of time as "leisure." I avoid the word. We tend to associate leisure with sheer rest and idleness. Naturally enough. When we are working regularly and earn some free time — vacation for instance — rest and idleness may be exactly what we want. But if you are looking ahead to anywhere from five to twenty-five years of extra time, you may want something a little more demanding. That could be almost anything — hobbies, physical activites, mental games, volunteering, community work, paid part-time work, or your own little enterprise. Let's call it a "future pursuit."*

Any future pursuit should be as enjoyable as so-called leisure. So if enjoyment is still the theme of your search, then you can follow some of the guidelines you used when you were entering or changing a career. The guidelines are basically the same in principal as STEPS 1 to 12 in the *Searchway*.

As an older person, you are not under as much pressure to come up with precise, immediate, and successful answers. Now you are looking for ideas and clues rather than exact outcomes. Consequently you will not want to wade through each STEP again. Most older people have found four high spots that should be reviewed (or tackled if it is the first time around). Although they echo four of the Searchway STEPS, we'll call them simply Assignments A, B, C, and D.

WARNING: When you complete Assignment D you will not necessarily have found the pot of gold at the end of the rainbow; but you will have informed or re-informed yourself on how to go after it.

A. Reviewing Your Life Experiences and Skills

First and foremost you should review your life experiences for the transkills you used. This is the same process you followed in STEPS 1 to 4 in Chapters 1 and 2. Take a look, too, at some recent experiences which you thoroughly enjoyed. Remember that an "experience" may simply be a task you performed in one of your activities. I cannot overemphasize the importance of reviewing experiences and skills. It sets you in motion. Witness some examples.

---

* If you have a future pursuit well in mind or underway and are sure you can follow it up, you will probably not be reading this chapter. My thoughts are addressed to those who are uncertain about what to do with their time or want to do something a little different.

A personnel manager who'd retired early came to a senior counseling center for part-time paid or volunteer work. Through his church he'd acquired an interest in working with the elderly. The other workshop members had all kinds of suggestions for him using his knowledge of employment to place older people on jobs. But his skills analysis had shown a strong current of getting pleasure from *helping people* in general. He broadened his search for a helping activity to include a hospital, where he volunteered as an orderly.

This is an oversimplified story. But this man's basic theme in life, *helping others*, emerged. He had used this transkill in the past in employment, church work, and care of the elderly. He chose to use it in the future in a new setting.

Checking out your skills can reassure you that your choice is sound.

A Polaroid pre-retiree in 1979 told a workshop about her life-long love of knitting. She had a vague idea about teaching it to children but was doubtful of her teaching ability. She also described her job as a quality control inspector. What she liked most about it was breaking in new employees. Only when she and the group began analyzing her craft and her work for skills did she see the connection. They both required *finger dexterity, handling small "tools," accuracy, patience, calculation,* and *working from precise instructions.* The fact that she liked teaching quality control procedures encouraged her with the idea of teaching knitting. Later she volunteered to teach knitting at a local senior citizen center.

Another quality control inspector (this in 1973) realized that performing strength tests and operating small equipment was not too much different from her craft of collecting and polishing stones; nor were these activites too different from a course she had recently taken in metal work.

Both employees had previously compartmentalized their hobbies and work. Now, they saw doors connecting the compartments. That connection gave continuity to their retirement.

Sometimes such a review bolsters those people who water down their assets.

A senior citizen came to a workshop to find something to do in her retirement. She said she didn't do much now, just baking, sewing, knitting, crocheting. "It's nothing. I've been doing it all my life." The group kept after her and discovered that her friends came to her for advice on recipes, patterns, and designs. She regularly won prizes at fairs. Within her circle she was an expert in the domestic arts. When the seminar ended I asked her what she'd learned. Quietly she replied, "I learned the things I do are important."

I hoped she had found the solution to her retirement "problem."

Some people find their perspectives broadened. Instead of seeing retirement as a limiting factor in life, they realize their opportunities are widened.

Jack, a machine operator, described creating string art designs. The group was impressed with his detailed description and the many skills involved like *manual, finger dexterity, attention to detail,* and especially the *making of something.* Later he was up front talking about the kick he got out of remodeling his porch. Someone suggested carpentry as a retirement project; another selling string art designs to order. He was not especially responsive. At the end he told us what he was thinking about. "I never realized how much these two things have in common. Now I can see I'm not restricted to string art or carpentry. There are a whole lot of other things I can do."

Occasionally an employee carves out a new future, yet remains right where he or she is.

Sara came to a workshop at an evening college because she was thinking about early retirement. She repaired typewriters all day at the customer service department of a typewriter manufacturer. Although she liked her job, the thought of seven more years appalled her. Her "experiences" were of a social nature, like volunteer committee work and politics.

Someone said: Sara, you sound like you're good at contacting people. Rapport, that's what you've got.

Sara: Oh, that's just my nature.

Someone else: Well, whatever you call it, you sure use it a lot.

And someone else again: Why won't they let you use it on your job?

The group had assignments. Sara decided hers was to ask the boss, "Could I work at the front counter handling customers once in a while?" She reported back that the boss had replied, "Let me think about it." Her vision of the next seven years suddenly changed.

For those who start thinking about the problem of retirement well in advance there may be the unexpected payoff in the discovery of a second career.

A manager of materials control who was thinking about early retirement quickly found clues that led him to accept an early retirement option and go into real estate at Lake Havasu City, Arizona. He wrote, "It's too bad I didn't identify my aptitude and latent skills sooner for this game I am now in. Had I gone into real estate 20 years ago I think I would have been a lot happier and a lot richer. Oh well, you can't win 'em all!"

Here was a person seriously considering bowing out from regular work who flipped himself into a new career.

Ideas for second careers; using old skills in new settings; confirming a choice; finding importance in what you already do; broadening your horizons; or finding new outlets right on site are all possible outcomes of assessing skills the way these people did.

B. Reviewing Your "Likes"

Assignment B is to dig out the likes and preferences you want to see more of in the future and can afford. Your source is the form you filled out in STEP 5 (p. 35) where you listed the things you like or like to do. Every older person has an amazing assortment of pleasant memories. Bring your list up to date, or make a new one. Then —

— place an "F" opposite those that you want as part of your future.

— place an "A" opposite those that cost nothing or that you can afford.

If you think about those that are coded both "F" and "A" you'll probably find numerous ideas worth looking into.

C. Dreaming the Impossible

The third assignment is much like the question you asked yourself in STEP 6 (p. 36) about a dream occupation. Here it is: Jot down something you would like to do if you had time, money, and no responsibilities. (Try to exclude sheer idleness.) Make it a daydream, if you want, or a wild idea. Don't make it too practical or realistic.

The far out idea of one engineer contemplating retirement was to travel to exotic places, take photos and notes, and develop travelogues for home consumption. He made it sound impossible because of the cost of travel. "Why can't you do all that closer to home?" someone queried. "Aren't there unusual subjects in the U.S.A. or even in New England?" He mulled it over, and later commented, "I'll have to think about that."

Thus your pie in the sky can be another rich source of ideas to look into. Once you've dreamed it, just figure out what part or parts you could realistically put into effect. Certainly, if it's *your* dream you are on safe ground bringing it down to earth.

D. Sampling a Future Pursuit

Your fourth move is to sample a pursuit you would like to know more about. These pursuits, remember, may be any kind of activity including part-time work or your own enterprise. Sampling this idea is like the exploration process described in STEP 12. You're not making a commitment yet, only an investigation.

You sample by first choosing a pursuit from the information in Assignments A, B, and C. From A you may find either an old or recent enjoyable experience that triggers an idea; reviewing your transkills may provide other clues. From Assignment B, check over the activities that you coded "F" for future, and "A" for affordable. Scrutinize your wild idea (Assignment C) with a view as to whether you can make it practical by lowering your sights. Pick some element of it that you could do something about.

Before dashing off to explore this pursuit, you should pause and consider what you already know about it. Invariably, I have found that people know a lot more about these ideas than they think. Following is a worksheet to help you assess the situation. This assessment is an essential part of the sampling process.

How one person at a pre-retirement planning session filled in this worksheet is shown on page 134.

The final question "WHEN?" is the hurdle for most of us. There is seldom any good reason why most people cannot start investigating a possibility immediately. But will they? Will the potential pianist open the Yellow Pages tonight and look for a piano warehouse? Will the photographer conjure up an unusual travelogue subject near at hand and try it out on a weekend or vacation? Will the air traffic controller who is retired early pursue his lifelong bent for "looking at houses" and take a course for his real estate broker's license? And by the same token would you or I?

We don't always know. Alas, the pull to put off and postpone is strong. We tend to wait until some event forces us to act. And if that event is the actual falling of the retirement ax we may then think it too late to act.

WORKSHEET

Sampling a Future Pursuit

Something I'd like to look into:

What transkills and talents do I already have for this?

What knowledge and know-how have I already acquired for this activity?

What do I lack at this point? What problems might there be?

If I want to pursue this idea, what do I need to do to overcome these lacks or problems?

When?

WORKSHEET

Sampling a Future Pursuit

Something I'd like to look into:

Playing The piano

What transkills and talents do I already have for this?

Finger dexterity, eye-hand-body coordination, memorizing being accurate, persistence, patience.

What knowledge and know-how have I already acquired for this activity?

I like listening to music and own many records.

What do I lack at this point? What problems might there be?

A piano and a teacher. Finding Them.

If I want to pursue this idea, what do I need to do to overcome these lacks or problems?

Price pianos of all sizes; ask for teachers in The area; find Them. Talk to Them about kind of music, lessons, fees, etc.

When?   *?*

I have no neat answer. But at least the knowledge that we have the map and compass to undertake explorations will help. Then we can start making our trials and errors well in advance so that when the deadline arrives we are ready to look forward to the 40 hours of new free time with enthusiasm.

RESOURCES

Planning for Free Time

Bolles, Richard N. *The Three Boxes of Life,* Berkeley: Ten Speed Press, 1978. Chapter 5, pages 335-395.

14

A Way of Life

You may feel I overstate when I suggest using the message of this book as a way of life. The concept that a person carries a portfolio of skills through a variety of situations from childhood to old age is hard to keep in the forefront. It is not manifest. The very fact that we use these transkills so flexibly tends to obscure them. They pale beside the knowledge-based skills we can easily identify — art, engineering, inn-keeping. At school and at work we learn to keep our eye on subject matter.

In the preceding six chapters I have indicated practical applications of the *Searchway* at stages in one's life — at home, school, work, and in retirement. These may seem like intermittent applications. But some people can articulate their lifetime themes in terms of a talent that blends with an overriding purpose.

Will Sampson is the six-foot five-inch American Indian who acted in "Cuckoo's Nest" and "Buffalo Bill." He has three loves — performing, directing, and painting; he discerns the parallel in all three. "You try to get people to see the same things in it that you do."[1]

Tony Pino masterminded the Brink's stick-up in Boston. He and his gang penetrated the Brink garage 75 times before he perfected the plan. One of his colleagues said: "Tony saw things no one else saw. He saw things like an artist sees things."[2] Tony would have agreed.

John Holt, the educator, says he had to learn to guess and bluff when as a novice cellist he began to play chamber music with musicians better than himself.[3] He wrote me that it took this same kind of risk-taking to go into the mail order book business and to live independently as a writer/publisher/lecturer rather than as a tenured teacher.

None of these is a graduate of the *Searchway*, but they hold personal philosophies that translate directly into the use of certain transkills. They are skilled respectively in —

— expressing to others what they see;

— seeing things others do not see;

— taking chances in starting up things that are needed.

Conversely, the people who read their skills correctly are able to develop philosophies of their own.

> One Columbia Business School graduate who had been through the skills analysis program returned to the career counseling office to review his "top successes." But they did not include being on the verge of heading up a $43 million affiliate. His successes from childhood on had been and remained in the realm of volunteer activity. He was confirming and reaffirming a philosophy of life: "The money does not interest me."[4]

Developing a life philosophy, though, may be overly ambitious; it is for most people. If you know what to do for the next 12 months, you figure you're lucky. If that is the case, you had better focus on maintaining your search for skills on a very current basis, week to week, month to month, or at least as the need arises.

There are also some other ways you can keep this approach alive for yourself and others. Opportunities often arise when people are talking about their future, whether near or distant. One situation is when you are in a position of responsibility for them, and the other when you are not.

Take the second situation when you are not responsible. That is, you have no official reason to concern yourself with someone's future. Yet the person makes a remark about what he or she might do. Regardless of how fleeting the comment may be, you have a single golden moment in which to be of help. As long as that person has raised the topic by mentioning it, you can legitimately ask, quite soon, a neutrally-phrased question about it. The question conveys your interest, not your bias. Some of the questions that further such interchanges are those that get the person thinking about the enjoyment and skills involved:

"What do you like about it specially?"

"Do you enjoy this kind of activity?"

"What kind of skills do you use?" (not 'need'); or

"Tell me more about what you said about photography."

The tone, conveying genuineness, is as important as the question. It must not convey the impression that you have your own answer to lay down. True, you may not get an answer that satisfies you. But relax. Your friend may later see that his or her answer was not the best, and take another bearing.

This posture of yours need not make you feel you are getting involved in professional counseling. But it does require a lot of restraint. You will have to persuade yourself that you can be more help letting other people seek their own solutions than by proferring yours; that their brains on the matter can produce a better idea than yours; that something is more likely to come from your question than from your answer to it. Finally, you will have to put aside the natural satisfaction you get from dispensing "helpful" advice.

All these attitudes are good traits of the professional counselor, but you do not have to be one to practise them. Often these opportunities to help are fleeting and brief. No matter. You can be effective as well as fleeting and brief if you follow these guidelines.

The other situation is when you do have responsibility or a leadership role, and you feel you should initiate something about the person's future. You might be thrust into the role some time as parent, older relative, child of aging parent, teacher, advisor, counselor, boss, or as an informal, ad hoc, temporary leader. Here the footing can be slippery. Now your words, whatever you say, however mildly, may be heard as the voice of authority. So watch out. You may get sucked into playing a role that at this moment is inappropriate.

As "leader" you are supposed to know the answers, so you are expected to give them. This might cause you to think that you should have some opinion about what this person should do with his or her life; then you might be tempted to voice it gratuitously.

Volunteering an opinion about another's future is risky. The subject belongs primarily to that individual, not to others. Your idea lacks some credibility because it is not that person's own.

Moreover, by introducing the topic first you may inhibit the very discussion you would like to see develop. The other person may find it hard to formulate his or her ideas out loud once you have stated or implied yours first. One tends to think twice before answering one's "leader." So if the individual is not ready, you are forcing him or her either to rebut your suggestion or duck it.

The guideline is to wait until the person makes some remark on the subject. However slight it may be, you then have the cue to pick up the topic. Your lead consists of the same kind of inquiry you made of your friend. It will be non-evaluative, non-aligned, yet caring. Again, don't argue about an answer you don't agree with. The person may not like the sound of it either, and may later reformulate it. He or she has thought out one answer, and is competent to think out an alternative. Your contribution is starting the chain of thought, not forging the final link.

If you are a leader in the professional sense of being a teacher, counselor, or boss, then Chapters 9 to 13 of Part II may have special use for you. You might feel, as I do, that people can be taught the process, and that your duties allow you the opportunity to do so. Granted, in these past chapters I am placing initiative for using *Searchway* ideas on the individual. I do not want him or her to count on getting too much help from the world at large of teachers, counselors, and employers.

But as you have gone through and absorbed the *Searchway*, you are in a position to try out some of the techniques in Part I on others. You should not feel compelled to follow the 12 STEPS in exact order and detail. If you are a teacher or counselor you may get ideas for their use in school, college, and finding work from Chapters 9, 10, and 11. If you are an employer, you and the personnel people can encourage applicants and employees to focus more on their transkills and what they enjoy, as described in Chapters 11 and 12.

I believe in one absolute requirement. It is that you start off with STEPS 1 to 4 — the listing and describing of your enjoyed experiences and the identifying of the transkills you used. These moves develop a force that energizes. It turns people away from dwelling on their limited education and work experience; it turns them towards their positive life experiences and thus towards their critical transferable skills. The basic principle emerges — we should shape our key life activities around things that we enjoy and that use our talents. If we are endowed with these talents, then surely we should make use of them.

FOOTNOTES

1. "Big Will," Newsweek, July 26, 1976.
2. Noel Behn, Big Stick-Up at Brink's (New York: Warner Books, 1977), pp. 277 and 303.
3. John Holt, Never Too Late: My Musical Life Story (New York: Delacorte/Seymour Lawrence, 1978), p. 171.
4. Richard M. Gummere Jr., "DIG/Columbia University's Program to Help Students Find Answers," Journal of College Placement, April-May 1972.

RESOURCES

Giving Advice

Levinson, Harry. "Management by Whose Objectives," Harvard Business Review, July-August 1970, p. 133.

Roethlisberger, F.J. and William J. Dickson. Management and the Worker. Cambridge: Harvard University Press, 1956, pp. 286-290.

Rogers, Carl R. Counseling and Psychotherapy. Boston: Houghton Mifflin, 1942. Pp. 118-126.

Rogers, Carl R. and F.J. Roethlisberger, "Barriers and Gateways to Communication," Harvard Business Review, Jy.-Aug. 1952, pp. 46-52.

Simon, Sidney B. and Sally Wendklos Olds. Helping Your Child Learn Right from Wrong. New York: Simon & Schuster, 1976. Ch. 15, "Clarifying Responses," pp. 157-161.

Index